DARK PEAK WALKS

About the Author

Paul Besley first went walking in the Dark Peak when he was 14 years old and a love of the high moors and gritstone edges was born. Over the following years he has explored the area, walking its moorlands, investigating hidden cloughs, expanding his knowledge and experience: he has learned when and where the Dark Peak is best and which are the best walks.

He is a volunteer ranger for the Peak District National Park and a member of Woodhead Mountain Rescue, an informative walking guide and writer. His ranger base is in the Upper Derwent Valley, just a few minutes from where he lives in Sheffield with his wife, metalsmith Alison Counsell, and their three dogs Olly, Monty and Scout.

For more information, Paul can be contacted at www.paulbesley.com.

DARK PEAK WALKS

40 WALKS EXPLORING THE PEAK DISTRICT GRITSTONE AND MOORLAND LANDSCAPES

by Paul Besley

JUNIPER HOUSE, MURLEY MOSS,
OXENHOLME ROAD, KENDAL, CUMBRIA LA9 7RL
www.cicerone.co.uk

© Paul Besley 2017
First edition 2017
ISBN-13: 978 1 85284 519 3
Reprinted 2019 (with updates)
Printed in China on behalf of Latitude Press Ltd.
A catalogue record for this book is available from the British Library.

1:50K route mapping © Crown copyright OS PU100012932.

1:100K route mapping by Lovell Johns www.lovelljohns.com.
© Crown copyright 2017 OS PU100012932.
NASA relief data courtesy of ESRI.

All photographs are by the author unless otherwise stated.

This book is dedicated to metalsmith Alison Counsell.
My wonderful wife, best friend, and fellow adventurer.
Thank you for everything. I love you dearly.

Updates to this guide

While every effort is made by our authors to ensure the accuracy of guidebooks as they go to print, changes can occur during the lifetime of an edition. Any updates that we know of for this guide will be on the Cicerone website (www.cicerone.co.uk/519/updates), so please check before planning your trip. We also advise that you check information about such things as transport, accommodation and shops locally. Even rights of way can be altered over time. We are always grateful for information about any discrepancies between a guidebook and the facts on the ground, sent by email to updates@cicerone.co.uk or by post to Cicerone, Juniper House, Murley Moss, Oxenholme Road, Kendal LA9 7RL.

Register your book: To sign up to receive free updates, special offers and GPX files where available, register your book at www.cicerone.co.uk.

Front cover: The Vale of Edale from Kinder Scout (Walk 39)

CONTENTS

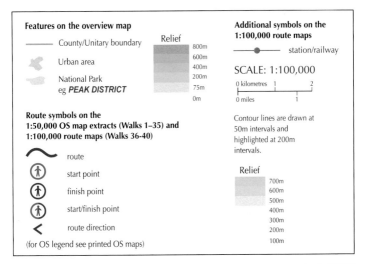

Features on the overview map

———— County/Unitary boundary

Urban area

National Park
eg **PEAK DISTRICT**

Relief

- 800m
- 600m
- 400m
- 200m
- 75m
- 0m

Route symbols on the
1:50,000 OS map extracts (Walks 1–35) and
1:100,000 route maps (Walks 36-40)

route

start point

finish point

start/finish point

route direction

(for OS legend see printed OS maps)

Additional symbols on the
1:100,000 route maps

———•——— station/railway

SCALE: 1:100,000

0 kilometres   1   2

0 miles   1

Contour lines are drawn at
50m intervals and
highlighted at 200m
intervals.

Relief

- 700m
- 600m
- 500m
- 400m
- 300m
- 200m
- 100m

Warning

Hill walking can be a dangerous activity carrying a risk of personal injury
or death. It should be undertaken only by those with a full understanding
of the risks and with the training and experience to evaluate them. While
every care and effort has been taken in the preparation of this guide, the
user should be aware that conditions can be highly variable and can change
quickly, materially affecting the seriousness of a high-level walk. Therefore,
except for any liability that cannot be excluded by law, neither Cicerone
nor the author accept liability for damage of any nature (including damage
to property, personal injury or death) arising directly or indirectly from the
information in this book.

The Dark Peak is prone to sudden changes of weather and the nature
of the upland areas demands a high level of navigational skill. Walkers
should be properly equipped for the conditions and leave details of their
route with an appropriate person. To call out Mountain Rescue, ring 999
or the international emergency number 112: this will connect you via any
available network. Once connected to the emergency operator, ask for the
police. Walkers can also avail of an emergency SMS system by registering
their phone with the provider.

Acknowledgments

I got to do the good bit: walking all the routes, finding out all the information. I was not alone; many people helped in producing this book.

First I would like to thank Mark Richards, without whose suggestion and help this book would never have happened. Of course, someone needs to sort out my words and print the book. Thank you to Jonathan Williams, Sian Jenkins, Natalie Simpson, Stephanie Rebello and the team at Cicerone.

Many people gave their time to check my routes and make the odd suggestion, and even walk some of the routes with me. To David and Stephanie Haffenden, Phil Newing, Duncan Sissons, Tony Amies, Alison Counsell, Gail Ferriman and Jeff Cole, thank you, for your assistance, your patience and encouragement, and above all your friendship.

I would like to thank the Area Rangers of the Peak District National Park, who gave me their time, advice and encouraging words: Paul Wetton, Tom Lewis, Fiona Draisey, Neil Hanshaw, Andy Valentine, Martin Winder, Steven Bell, Gordon Danks and Richard Pett of Aldern House. Also thanks to Debra Wilson, who talked so enthusiastically about Moors For The Future and helped to explain what it all meant; to Michelle Sullivan from the National Trust High Peak Estate, who provided me with so much helpful information; and to Paul Bridge and Mike Potts, who provided information about the aircraft crash sites.

But most important of all, thanks to my wife Alison Counsell for supporting me throughout the project, and giving endless encouragement. I owe everything to you.

Long Causeway and Stanage Edge

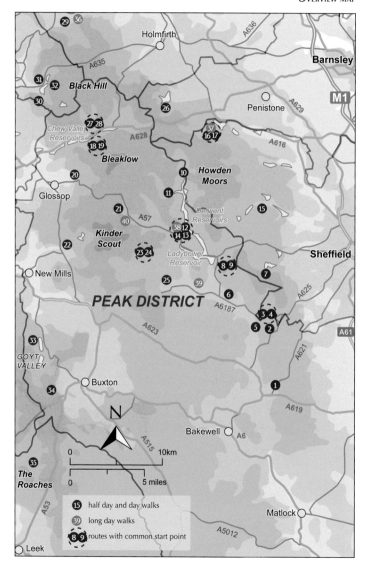

Holmfirth

Barnsley

M1

Black Hill

Penistone

Chew Valley
Reservoirs

Bleaklow

Howden
Moors

Glossop

Darwent
Reservoirs

Kinder
Scout

Ladybower
Reservoir

Sheffield

New Mills

PEAK DISTRICT

GOYT
VALLEY

A61

Buxton

N

Bakewell

0   10km

0   5 miles

The
Roaches

Matlock

Leek

15 half day and day walks

39 long day walks

8 9 routes with common start point

Walking along the Great Ridge (Walk 25)

INTRODUCTION

Full winter kit on Kinder Scout (Walk 24)

On a beautiful winter's day with a sky that was powder blue and dotted with brilliant white clouds, I dropped down from Barrow Stones to Ridgewalk Moor. As the path levelled out the wind suddenly became stronger, not enough to blow me over, but enough for me to think it was time to be getting off the high moor and down into the valley. The afternoon was drawing to a close and my walk that day had been one of the most enjoyable that winter. I hadn't seen a soul, it being a weekday, and my walk had taken me off the footpath and across a succession of moors, rising up to Bleaklow Stones via a series of spot heights that formed a natural ascent. As I turned to head towards Round Hill I had the most amazing sense of the ocean. I stopped and breathed in the air, taking huge draughts into my lungs. I could smell and taste sea salt on the wind, fresh, tangy and exhilarating. It is a moment I relive, and it is just one of many memories that I have of the Dark Peak.

The area has a habit of producing days that are to be remembered; it is one of the reasons it is loved by so many people. It is a place of great beauty and variety, with a landscape that changes with the seasons. Its primary trait is one of restrained menace. The land broods, waiting for an excuse to show its dark side, often suddenly from nowhere and in a most brutal way. There is a reason why seven Mountain Rescue teams surround the Dark Peak, which alone is enough of a warning to any walker to treat the area with respect.

The Dark Peak is fringed with gritstone edges that look out across wide valleys to high peat moorland. It is famous for two things. The first is gritstone, coarse sandstone laid down between 360 million and 300 million years ago when the area was a vast river delta. The gritstone forms long high edges, a Mecca for climbers, and outcrops that give walkers superb viewpoints across wide valleys to the high moors beyond. The second feature the Dark Peak is famous for is encountered by all who venture onto the high moors: peat. In summer, it takes the form of a dark chocolate brownie that has a gentle bounce which makes a gait slightly comical. In wet weather it is an entirely different matter. Chocolate fondant is perhaps an appropriate description. Peat, when saturated, still maintains its solid appearance, which makes crossing the moors a challenge, especially if you enter a grough, a steep-sided incision from which egress is less than noble. At best you can end up covered in the black ooze up to your knees; at worst it can be up to your thighs.

The walks are not just about this incredible landscape. They are also about the human element that lies deep within the Dark Peak. From the Neolithic remains of fire platforms to

Peat is one of the Dark Peak's characteristics

Bronze Age cairns and burial mounds, we walk in footsteps long ago imprinted into the soft peat. It is an area that has witnessed murder, with the martyrs at Padley Chapel (Walk 5), mystery at Cutthroat Bridge (Walk 8), and human despair in Hannah Mitchell, who lived a life under such cruelty at Alport Hamlet, yet went on to become a Manchester magistrate and writer (Walk 13). The first national park to be granted this status was the Peak National Park, in April 1951, with those who fought for the Right to Roam frequently at the forefront of the national parks campaign.

Industry has made its mark, first with the peat cutting and then more visibly along the gritstone edges and the quarries producing the famous millstones and the stone for the great dams. War also has played its part, with at least three areas taking part in military training, the most famous being the Dambusters of the Upper Derwent Valley. In the last century the area has been the resting place of many aircraft, the remains of which can still be seen.

The Dark Peak presents a different experience with each season. Autumn invites you to savour the blazing colours of the ancient woodlands around Longshaw, and the smell of the landscape readying for the winter slumber. Then take a winter's walk on Higger Tor, the wind driving snow horizontally across the moor, the cold biting the cheeks: perhaps you will be lucky enough to experience the thrill of sighting a mountain hare in its white winter cloak. In spring the path up to Grindle Barn from Ladybower has a beautiful meadow full of cornflowers and buttercups. And finally summer beckons, promising long days exploring the groughs of the Kinder Scout plateau, lunch at Crowden Head, reclining on soft sweet-smelling grass, and bathing in the Fairie Pools at Slippery Stones after a hard day's walking. There are ample opportunities for challenge and character-building, testing navigational skill and self-reliance, and endless moments of pleasure discovering this rich and varied landscape.

I hope you enjoy the walks in this book and that it leads to further exploration of the Dark Peak and some wonderful memories.

GEOLOGY

The Peak District is formed mainly of gritstone, which sits above a limestone bed. In the southern part of the Peak District, the White Peak, the gritstone has eroded away leaving the white limestone formed some 360 million years ago now visible on the surface. In the north and on the eastern and western fringes, the gritstone remains in place on the surface giving us the Dark Peak.

The gritstone of the Dark Peak was formed in the Carboniferous Period around 360–300 million years ago at a time of fluctuating sea levels due to ice melt. The gritstone of the

Dark Peak, primarily made from sandstone and grit, was laid down when the area was a huge river delta that poured sediment from the north over the smooth limestone rock, resulting in the formation of gritstone rock, often in layers or strata. Between the layers can be found thin seams of shale and coal, formed from decaying plant material during periods of warmer weather.

Gritstone has a coarse surface that is harder than the limestone or shales upon which it sits. Layering of the gritstone deposits has produced horizontal banding while weathering has produced vertical fissures. This gives a distinctive look of long edges running in straight lines, with the edge interspersed with buttresses of horizontal layers separated by vertical cracks, as seen at Stanage Edge. Where harder sandstone deposits are present, erosion has resulted in gritstone tors where the surrounding softer stone has been weathered away. This is seen most clearly on Derwent Edge and Kinder Scout.

The shale formed from mud that lies deeper than the sandstone and grit can be found interspersed within a line of gritstone, the most easily visible being at Mam Tor, where gritstone sits above the shale at the base of the mountain. As shale breaks up easily this makes it a very unstable material and, as in Mam Tor, can produce significant landslips. Thin seams of coal are seldom visible but these remains of plant material laid down during warmer spells of the Carboniferous Period can be seen around Derbyshire Bridge and also in the Longdendale Valley.

Peat, formed from plant material some 10,000 years ago, sits behind the gritstone edges and on the slopes down into the valley at a depth of up to four metres. On the high moorlands the peat has been eroded, producing deep incisions called groughs where it has been eroded down to the underlying bedrock. This came about partially through natural processes but also through deliberate human activity. In the 19th and 20th century drains were cut into the peat in an attempt to make the moors drier for agricultural purposes. The effect of such drainage was to reduce the moors' ability to hold water and also to take sediment from the moor down into the valleys. New peat could not be generated from rotting material, further reducing the moors' water-retention abilities and affecting the delicate natural balance of plant and wildlife where drainage had occurred. Along with the peat, the Dark Peak is one of the world's most important sites for blanket bog. Blanket bog enables the growth of plants such as sphagnum moss, a key plant for the production of new peat. The Moors For The Future Project seeks to reverse the damage caused by moorland peat erosion and promotes the development of new peat by the seeding of grasses, sphagnum moss and other plantlife that will increase the moors' capacity to

The Wheel Stones or Coach and Horses (Walk 12)

produce new peat material. The peat is also a major component of flood defences for the surrounding cities, the moor holding water for longer periods to allow floodwater to disperse without damaging settlements downstream.

Groughs should not be confused with cloughs, which are deeply incised valleys running down the hillside from the plateau above. They invariably have a stream running along the length that is cutting deeper into the hillside; many have waterfalls.

PLANTS AND WILDLIFE

Plant and wildlife within the Dark Peak is diverse. The high moorlands have a wide range of grasses and sedges, bilberry and crowberry and cottongrass, as well as managed bracken and heather. There is little tree cover except for the occasional rowan and conifer. The mountain hare is a common sight, as are grouse, which are heavily managed for sport shooting. Deer are also present on the Eastern Moors. Around the gritstone edges merlins, peregrine falcons, goshawks, hen harriers and buzzards may be spotted. Curlew, golden plover and dippers frequent the moors and valleys, while the common lizard and the adder may be found basking on moorland paths.

Grouse moors have a cover of heather, managed to produce differing habitats suitable for the life-cycle of the red grouse. Three main types

15

Cottongrass blowing in the soft breeze

of heather can be found in the Dark Peak; the most ubiquitous is common heather that produces the purple blankets of late summer that the Dark Peak is famous for.

Ancient woodlands of oak, birch, rowan, holly and hazel can be found on the valley slopes and in the valley bottoms. Bluebells, wood anemone and wood sorrel are abundant, as is the pungent wild garlic along the bottom of the valley. Many of the valley sides were planted with conifer as a commercial crop. Where it is practical these are now being replaced with natural woodlands. The National Trust has also started a programme to introduce natural woodlands onto the steep slopes immediately below the high moors.

Farming is an important activity in the Dark Peak and farms cover the high moorlands as well as the lower slopes and valley bottoms. Sheep are the most common farm animal but there are cattle as well. Farmland is characterised by a drystone wall of medium size enclosing green pasture. In recent years Highland cattle have been used to control bracken, particularly on the Eastern Moors.

HISTORY

Ancient history

The area has long been inhabited by man and there is a great deal of evidence to be found on all the walks. Man's first appearance was during the

Neolithic period, some 10,000 years ago, evidenced by burial mounds, particularly on high viewpoints such as Pike Low, built around 2500BC. Bronze Age burial chambers and cairns are also common. A good place to view these is Bamford Moor (Walk 8) or the Eastern Moors (Walk 3).

The Romans and Normans
Roman occupation has left its imprint on the landscape as well, with several of the walks using Roman roads, and of course, there were the forts at Hope (Walk 39) and Glossop (Walk 20). The Peak District was of interest to the Romans due to its central location within the country and the lead deposits that would provide a good source of the mineral for lead work in piping and guttering.

The Normans arrived in AD1086 at the settlement of Pechesers (literally translated as Peak's Arse or Peak's Tail), now known as Castleton. There, William Peveril, son of William the Conqueror, built Peveril Castle above Cave Dale as a stronghold and means of increasing his power and control over the area, while also serving as a prison for offenders. The site of the castle gave the Normans control of the Peak Forest, which stretched from the Derwent Valley in the northeast to the Goyt Valley in the west, including a large area of what is now the Dark Peak.

The enclosures
The 13th century witnessed the first major change to the landscape in the form of enclosures. Enclosure removed land from the community

A fine example of a stone circle on Bamford Moor (Walk 8)

and placed it in the hands of the Lords and those who controlled areas of population. The primary reason for enclosure was profit from improved agricultural activities. The people who tended to lose out were the labourers and landless who were forced off the land and often into the towns. The first areas of land to be enclosed were those close to settlements and these can be easily identified as long narrow fields with straight boundaries. The next enclosures were more regular, rectangular shapes further up the valley slopes. The final enclosures occurred much later in the 19th century with the high moorlands being enclosed for sheep farming. Again, these are easily identified by very long stone walls that seem to stretch forever and lead nowhere useful!

The Industrial Revolution

Industry within the Dark Peak has been centred on the main areas of habitation. The very nature of the land and its geology precluded most mining activities, with the exception of small-scale coal mining on the western fringes and in the Longdendale Valley. It was not until the 17th century that industrial activity on a large scale became common. The availability of water powerful enough to work textile mills lead to the area becoming an important producer of cotton and woollen cloth, especially over on the western edge, which was bounded by the great industrial base of Lancashire. The position of the Dark Peak in the middle of the country and the plentiful supply of gritstone resulted in the export of stone wheels for milling flour and other crushing processes. Gritstone proved itself to be a good milling material but an even better source of building material, making it very attractive to the growing cities that surrounded the Dark Peak.

The ballooning population of the cities also led to an increased demand for water. The answer was the huge reservoirs; for a time the longest single chain in the world was in Longdendale (Walk 18). The reservoirs of the Upper Derwent Valley were completed in the 20th century and supplied much of the Midlands and Sheffield. As industry's reliance on water power diminished, the rivers returned to being habitats for wildlife. The water companies are now major landholders, owning much of the land around the reservoirs. Originally the land was bought to safeguard the quality of the water; now it is seen as a major recreational asset.

The rise of national parks

The 19th and 20th centuries brought about big changes to the uplands and moors. Enclosures had taken what was once common land from the people and placed it into the hands of wealthy individuals. Originally it had been for sheep grazing, enabling large herds to be grazed at little cost. The introduction of red grouse for sport shooting shifted the economic balance: sheep did not bring in the

Derwent Reservoir in the autumn (Walk 12)

same amount of income per hectare as red grouse, so the sheep and sheep farmers were removed and replaced with the grouse and gamekeeper. Enclosure also restricted access onto the moors and the introduction of shooting moors curtailed access for the vast majority of people. At a time when working classes were gaining a better standard of living, enabling them to travel and explore the countryside, they were prevented from doing so by private landowners. In conjunction, the political landscape was changing and a more socially inclusive attitude was developing. The fact that the high moors of the Dark Peak were closed to public access particularly annoyed and irritated the walkers of Manchester and Sheffield and it brought about a series of trespasses.

The most famous of these was the Mass Trespass of 1932 (Walk 22),

when hundreds of walkers walked up onto Kinder Scout against the wishes of the Duke of Devonshire and the instructions of the police. As a result of that day six people were tried and five were convicted of trespass and imprisoned. After the war various reports were produced on social matters. Arthur Hobhouse, a Liberal politician, produced a report in 1947 proposing the establishment of a series of national parks and detailing their uses. This resulted in the National Parks and Access to the Countryside Act of 1949, establishing 12 national parks across the country. They were chosen because of their outstanding natural beauty and unique identity. The first to open was the Peak National Park, now Peak District National Park, on 17 April 1951.

You may think mass trespasses are long in the past, but that is not the case. The last mass trespass to take place in the Dark Peak took place in 1985 on Bamford Moor (Walk 8), as this was closed to the public unless they had the permission of the landowner. Today that is not the case. The Countryside and Rights of Way Act of 2000 finally gave walkers the right to walk unfettered on open access land. There is, of course, a fly in the ointment. Landowners have the right to close their land to the public by giving special notice for a limited number of

AIRCRAFT CRASH SITES

B29 Superfortress wreckage (Walk 20)

The Dark Peak has an unusual and sad side. There are a large number of aircraft crash sites upon the high moors: many are military, a few are civilian. Remnants of the planes are still easily visible at many of the sites; others there is just a change in the landscape. Due to the flat nature of the high moorlands, especially Bleaklow, Kinder and Howden, navigational problems were encountered in poor weather and bad visibility. Misjudging the height, many planes simply hit the moorland, spreading wreckage and debris over a wide area. The sites are often used as a navigation exercise and are of historical interest. The earliest crash happened in 1918. The most famous and frequented one is on Bleaklow (Walk 20), where a USAF B29 crashed and has left extensive debris. As it was a military flight a service is now held each year on Remembrance Day. Grid references to sites that are near the walks can be found in Appendix C. Should you choose to visit any of the sites, please be respectful and do not remove any material.

days per year. If you are walking on the moors it is always worth checking to see whether there are any closures. It may well be due to sport shooting.

THE FUTURE

The Dark Peak is a unique landscape within Britain and as such is designated as a National Character Area with a Special Protection Area and a Special Area of Conservation, and almost 50 per cent of the National Character Area has been designated as Sites of Special Scientific Interest.

Today, many agencies are involved in the conservation of the area, ensuring that it remains special for generations to come. The National Trust, the RSPB, the Peak District National Park, the Wildlife Trust and Moors For The Future are changing the landscape, providing new woodlands of indigenous species and increasing the diversity of plants and wildlife.

The National Trust now owns large areas and its High Peak Estate and the Marsden Estates cover a large proportion of the Dark Peak. The Trust has a 50-year plan to promote and encourage care of this special landscape. They will develop healthy blanket bogs to increase the production of new peat and also trap millions of tonnes of carbon that would otherwise escape into the atmosphere. The plan calls for an increase in the diversity of wildlife and birds of prey, along with the planting of thousands of native shrubs and trees in the valleys and cloughs.

The water companies, Yorkshire Water, Severn Trent Water and United Utilities, are encouraging people to visit the reservoirs and surrounding moors for recreational purposes, building trails and infrastructure to enable everyone to enjoy this unique landscape. At the same time they are working to increase the diversity of wildlife and plants in the woodlands and on the moors that surround their operations.

Probably the biggest single project for the Dark Peak to date is the one being carried out by Moors For The Future: the restoration of the peat landscape. Repairing the damage done by years of industrial pollution from the surrounding cities will take time, energy and money, but the agency is bringing it back to life. The first stage is the seeding of grasses to lock in the peat that is still there. Then sphagnum moss seedlings are spread across the peat, taking root and holding water. When these rot down they will form new peat, and Moors For The Future intend to fill in the peat groughs (deep channels in the peat formed by erosion) by building thousands of small dams to hold back water and restore the landscape. These will also lock in carbon and increase the water-retention capacities of the peat, helping the atmosphere and saving communities downstream from flooding. By promoting tree and shrub growth in the cloughs they will also increase the quality of the water, reducing the need for

Dams across the groughs regenerating peat (Walk 32)

extensive cleaning operations. Due to the agency's activities the moors now have greater diversity of plantlife and wildlife, giving a whole new experience when walking across the land.

The Dark Peak is a major source of enjoyment and recreation for people who use the area. From walkers to climbers, mountain bikers, photographers, runners, bird watchers and people who just sit and enjoy this landscape, it has plenty to offer everyone.

LOCAL SERVICES AND TRANSPORT

The Dark Peak sits predominantly within the Peak District National Park. This was Britain's first national park, established on 17 April 1951. There are National Park Visitor Centres at Castleton, Edale and the Upper Derwent Valley, as well as ranger offices throughout the area. Details of all these and useful contacts can be found at www.peakdistrict.gov.uk.

Transport to and from the walks is more frequently by car and bike these days, but public transport is still available either by bus or train. The main Sheffield to Manchester rail line runs through the centre of the Dark Peak and is a useful means of accessing the area, with stations at Grindleford, Hathersage, Bamford, Hope, Edale and New Mills. Glossop and Marsden also have stations for access to the more remote areas. Transport by bus is obtainable from Sheffield, Manchester, Derby and Buxton. For details visit www.peakdistrict.gov.uk/visiting/publictransport.

The north of the Peak District has fewer and less frequent transport connections, so please take time to ensure that transport is available, especially at the end of a walk.

The central section of the Dark Peak contains the major centres of commerce and residence. Hathersage, Castleton, Glossop and Marsden all have shops, bars, restaurants and accommodation, making them good bases for the walks. Once away from these areas there is little available, which is part of the attraction of the Dark Peak. Therefore it is wise to take plenty of food and drink along on the walks. Details of accommodation and events can be found at www.visitpeakdistrict.com.

THE WALKS

The walks cover the whole of the Dark Peak. Some will be new to readers, others may be old friends. The book splits the Dark Peak into areas, each having a range of walks from short to long, some with more ascent than others. The shorter walks can be used as an introduction to each area, giving a brief taste of what is on offer. The medium-length walks offer a good day of walking that is not too taxing, while the longer walks are for those who want to lose the thronging crowds in the valley below and experience a true moorland wilderness experience.

There are some steep climbs in the Dark Peak and some of these are included in the walks to get the

Walking up Grindsbrook (Walk 24)

blood pumping. Some ascents tend to be gentler giving the walker time to look around, which is a joy because this is a landscape of high wide vistas and big skies, especially on the high moorlands.

RESPONSIBLE WALKING

Many of the walks are over grouse moors. These are highly managed environments specifically designed for the production of grouse for sport shooting. As such the landowners have the right to close a moor for public safety and the protection of the grouse and other ground-nesting birds. The landowner may also exclude dogs entirely from the moor or with certain exceptions. It is useful to check whether the moor has been closed or if there are any restrictions. This information can be found on the Natural England CRoW website at www.openaccess.naturalengland.org.uk.

Walking in the Dark Peak also brings a responsibility to ensure that no damage comes to the moor or the plant and wildlife by our actions. A moorland fire in May 2016, resulting from a portable barbeque being carelessly left behind, caused extensive damage to the heather and the destruction of much wildlife. Please act responsibly when on the moor: do not have open fires or barbeques, do not discard cigarettes or leave litter. Please follow the countryside code and remember to leave only footprints and take only photos and memories.

Big skies in the Dark Peak (Walk 7)

A rainbow on Barrow Stones (Walk 11)

MAPS AND NAVIGATION

All walks have been plotted using Ordnance Survey online mapping tools. The main paper maps for the area are the OS Explorer Dark Peak OL1 and White Peak OL24. Harvey and the BMC Dark Peak maps are also useful. Always take a map and compass, even if you are using a GPS device.

A word of caution: do not underestimate the area. Walking on the high moors – Bleaklow, Kinder Scout, Derwent and Howden – requires excellent navigation skills, especially in winter. It also requires good equipment and a knowledge of how to use it, and clothing that is appropriate to the time of year. The use of walking poles when crossing moorland can be helpful for maintaining balance and forward motion. They can also be useful when descending some of the steeper sections of the walks.

Smartphones can prove invaluable, especially when combined with a mapping app. However, these do drain the batteries, so be careful. One advantage of having a smartphone should you get into difficulty and need assistance from Mountain Rescue is its ability to let the teams know where you are, making rescue a much easier and quicker process. It is therefore advantageous to carry one of these devices for emergency purposes.

USING THIS GUIDE

The book is split into areas running from the east over to the west. The

25

walks were researched that way and it seemed a logical way of progressing. The first walk, from Chatsworth, is a gentle introduction to Dark Peak walking. The last, along the Roaches, ends the tour of the Dark Peak in the most magical way, looking out over England and on into Wales, a huge flat plain spread out before you. Perhaps you will pick an area and explore it. The walks have been kept as far away from each other as possible to allow for a fresh experience on each walk, and the routes stay as far from roads as possible also. This could have limited some walks, however, so some road walking is necessary on certain routes. Some walks can be cut short, such as the one from Grindleford to Higger Tor (Walk 5). There is so much to see and explore on all of the walks; there is nothing wrong in just walking to a particular feature and returning along the same path.

There is no perfect time to do the walks. The beauty of the Dark Peak is that it will serve you up a different experience every single time. It is recommended that you do the walks again and again and at different times of year for the full effect.

This guide includes an overview map and a route summary table. Use these in conjunction with the walk introduction at the beginning of each walk to select a suitable walk or series of walks. Timings are my walk times and do not include stopping for photographs, tea, ice creams or any other such comestible, getting lost or taking wrong turns. I have been generous with time, as there is no reason to rush across this magnificent landscape. The refreshments listed in the information boxes are those which are passed on the walk; in some cases there will be other pubs and cafés nearby.

In addition to the guide, taking the Ordnance Survey Explorer Maps OL1 Dark Peak and OL24 White Peak is recommended. The place names and features marked in **bold** within the walk descriptions refer to places featured on the maps contained within the guide. These maps are based on OS 1:50000, with the exception of the five longer walks (Walks 36-40), which are 1:100000. The mapping within the guide is intended to complement and not replace the correct OS Explorer map. There are many additional place names and features included throughout the route descriptions which are labelled on the OS 1:25000 maps.

If you use a GPS-enabled device to navigate, GPX files are available for free download at www.cicerone.co.uk/519/GPX.

EASTERN DARK PEAK

Higger Tor from Mother Cap (Walk 5)

The Eastern Dark Peak forms the eastern flank of the gritstone cap that stretches from Chatsworth in the south to Stanedge Pole in the central area of the Dark Peak. It is an area characterised by gritstone edges. The edges face the Derwent Valley, carved by wind, rain and ice, and make for long walks with wonderful views across the Dark Peak and into White Peak limestone country. The gritstone edges provided stone wheels for milling and crushing and form part of the Peak District National Park's identity. They are full of archaeological remains and industrial interest. The hand of man is much in evidence.

The moors that sit around the edges have wide views and big open skies, and are full of wildlife. Red deer, merlin and curlew are much in evidence, adders can be found basking in the sun on moorland paths, and hares can be seen running through the grass. The walking is easy, with fewer groughs to navigate than in the central and northern areas of the Dark Peak.

WALK 1
Chatsworth to Birchen Edge

Start/Finish	Chatsworth House SK 259 702
Distance	17.5km (11 miles)
Ascent	455m
Time	5hrs
Terrain	Steep, uneven ground, open moor and forest tracks
Map	OS 1:25000 Explorer OL24 White Peak
Refreshments	Chatsworth House
Parking	Chatsworth House SK 259 702

Chatsworth is a wonderful place to start and end a walk. The grounds reflect an interesting period of English social history, full of the romance and adventure of the European tours of the landed gentry. The Three Ships on Birchen Edge provide a wonderful photo opportunity with extensive views across Chatsworth. Hob Hurst's House is an important site, being one of the first to be protected by law. The end of the walk brings you through the grounds surrounding Chatsworth House and provides stunning views over gardens created by Capability Brown and Joseph Paxton.

From Chatsworth House car park walk directly west to **Queen Mary's Bower**, a folly situated by the River Derwent. Take the tarmac drive north past the nursery and on to the Cannon kissing gate to exit the park and enter **Baslow** by a walled lane. At the road junction turn left onto the A619, then cross it at the pelican crossing and walk up the road directly opposite for 400 metres. Where the road forks take the right hand road uphill, continuing on when the road becomes the track Bar Road and pass through a Peak District National Park access gate to a stony track leading up towards Baslow Edge. At the top do not go left to Baslow Edge but proceed straight on to **Wellington's Monument**.

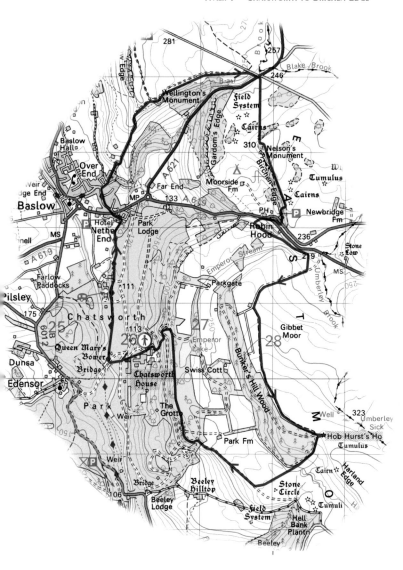

Wellington's Monument, Baslow Edge

The stone cross is **Wellington's Monument**, erected in honour of the Duke of Wellington. It looks across the valley to Nelson's Monument on Birchen Edge, met later in the walk. The large boulder visible on the moor above Baslow Edge is the Eagle Stone. Bouldering routes on the stone include: The Beagle Has Landed, The Good The Bad and The Beagle, and A Beagle Too Far.

Follow the northeast track from the monument, eventually bounded by a stone wall on the left and passing a guide stoop on the right, to a gate giving access to a minor road. Go right and then straight across the **A621** and through a wooden gate on the opposite corner of the crossroads. Initially the path across the open moor is flagged but it becomes faint, winding its way for 850 metres south to a very large boulder situated on the right in a clearing among trees below the gritstone edge. This marks the turning point to go left and make a short easy scramble up onto **Birchen Edge**. Reaching the triangulation pillar at the top, head southeast to three large gritstone boulders on the left known as the Three Ships. ▶

This is a good place to stop for refreshments.

Nelson's Monument stands by three of his ships: Victory, Defiance and Royal Soverin, the last spelled incorrectly. The obelisk was erected 56 years before Wellington's Monument.

If time allows make a diversion to Gardom's Edge to view a menhir (standing stone) and also a replica of a stone with cups and rings. It is well worth the effort.

Follow the footpath along the edge for approximately 700 metres until it turns sharp right by two concrete posts marking the position of a pipeline. Follow the path right, down the steep slope, to reach a wide path with a wall beyond. Turn left and walk south down the path, keeping the wall on your right, to a gate that leads onto a

The Three Ships on Birchen Edge

road taking you past a **pub**. From the pub walk down the A619 pavement until you are opposite a signpost on the other side of the road pointing to a concessionary path to Chatsworth. Cross here and go over the stile, down the stone steps and across a wooden bridge, then up a short slope to a marker post.

Turn left and walk along a waymarked footpath, following the signposts at all times southeast to stone steps set into a wall. Go over the wall and continue following the marker posts leading you up a small clough with a stream on your left until you reach a marker post at the foot of a slope. Turn right here and walk up the slope and out onto open moorland. Follow the footpath across the moor to go through a gate giving access onto a wide track. Turn right along the track following it across **Gibbet Moor** to woodland in the distance. Walk on past the woodland until it finishes at the corner of a wall. Go straight on, east, for 70 metres to **Hob Hurst's House**.

> **Hob Hurst's House** was one of the first monuments in Britain to be protected under the Ancient Monuments Act, a fact noted by the stone bollards with the inscription VR for Queen Victoria. It is a large burial cairn that contained burnt human remains.

Retrace your steps to the wall corner and turn left to descend the slope keeping the walled forest plantation on your right. Where the plantation ends and the wall turns northwest carry straight on southwest across Rabbit Warren to meet a well-made track. Turn right, northwest, along the track and follow this until it ends at a wall stile leading into woodland. Go over the stile and along the woodland track until it forks after crossing a stream. Take the left hand fork and follow the track until the junction with a tarmac forest road. Walk straight across the road and proceed along a woodland track bearing left at the next track junction. Pass the Cascade Waterfall stopping to take in the views across Chatsworth Gardens and carry on to the Hunting Tower.

*The Hunting Tower
Chatsworth*

Bess of Hardwick had the **Hunting Tower** built both as a retreat and to view hounds hunting deer in the park. Lancelot Capability Brown turned the deer park into one of his creations embodying coherence and elegance.

From the Hunting Tower go down the steps situated beyond the cannons, cross the track at the foot of the steps and then descend steep stone steps and a footpath to connect with a forest track. Go left along the track and at the next track junction go right and right again at the next junction, then follow the track down to re-enter the car park.

WALK 2

Longshaw Estate and the gritstone edges

Start/Finish	Longshaw Lodge SK 264 799
Distance	14km (9 miles)
Ascent	300m
Time	4hrs
Terrain	Moorland and woodland footpath
Map	OS 1:25000 Explorer OL24 White Peak
Refreshments	Longshaw Estate Café
Parking	Longshaw Estate SK 266 800

This classic walk along gritstone edges starts at Longshaw Lodge, a former shooting lodge of the Dukes of Rutland, and follows old estate trails to White Edge, returning to the Longshaw Estate via Curbar and Froggatt Edges.

The edges have long been favoured climbing crags, with Froggatt having hundreds of routes along its length including the enigmatically named Valkyrie and Jump Before You Look. The area is teeming with wildlife including larger red deer, water voles, ring ouzels, curlew, merlin and buzzard, and the walk takes you through oak woodlands and wildflower meadows.

From the main drive of Longshaw Lodge take the track that goes to the left of the café through woodland and curves to the right behind the building. Proceed through the gate onto a grassed track and continue along until the track forks. Take the left hand route, the way forward eventually signalled by a large pole, to reach a gate leading onto the junction of three roads. This area is known as Wooden Pole.

The base of the **pole** is dated 1778, the pole marking parish boundaries and also acting as a waymark for the old packhorse route that crossed this part of the area. The original line of the route is along the grassed track you have just walked up, the road being enclosed by the Duke of Rutland.

Go through the gate and cross the junction to a second gate straight ahead giving access to White Edge Moor. Walk down the track towards a tall house, **White Edge Lodge**, situated on your right. Turn left at the house and ascend to a gate in the wall at the edge of **White Edge Moor**. Keep an eye out for the herd of red deer to your left on Big Moor. With binoculars, the large stags are easy to spot; it takes time and patience to see the others.

Go through the gate and then head right, directly south, along a track to White Edge. Continue along **White Edge** until you reach a **triangulation pillar**, then 200 metres further along take the footpath down off the edge, to the moorland below, heading for two large walled enclosures with many internal divisions. On reaching the enclosures take the path between the two and follow the right hand wall around to reach a road and **car park**. Go through the gate and across the car park to a gate on your right that will lead you up onto **Curbar Edge**.

The footpath takes you along both Curbar Edge and **Froggatt Edge**, eventually ending in a short descent to a gate giving access onto the A625. Go right for 50 metres

White Edge Lodge

up the road and then cross to a stile over a wall on the opposite side. Go over the stile, descending to a stream, before going up to **The Haywood** where the path forks. Take the left fork to stay on a reasonably level footpath that leads through a gate into a lane with a wooden fence on the left and culminating in a junction with a road.

Turn right along the road and immediately after a house on your right take a signposted footpath right up a tarmac drive to a gate by a house. Go through the gate and continue up the driveway to a footpath that eventually leads through woodland to a gate in a wall. Go through this gate and turn left along a wide track with walls on either side then follow the left hand wall down to a stream. Cross the stream and ascend the hill opposite then cross open moorland with a wall on your left to a stile leading onto a track. Turn left

and follow the track through **Longshaw Estate** to return to **Longshaw Lodge**.

Triangulation pillar on White Edge

The **Longshaw Estate** is the former country shooting estate of the Dukes of Rutland. Longshaw Lodge was built in the early 1800s as a shooting box, and drives were put in the estate to facilitate ease of movement for shoots, the most prominent of which is the bridleway under Burbage Rocks. The estate has ancient woodlands with fast flowing streams in deep gorges, such as Padley Gorge, traditional oak woodlands and meadow, gritstone edges and outcrops, and a wealth of history.

WALK 3

Fox House to Big Moor

Start/Finish	Fox House Inn SK 267 802
Distance	18km (11 miles)
Ascent	310m
Time	5hrs
Terrain	Open moorland, footpaths and tracks
Map	OS 1:25000 Explorer OL24 White Peak
Refreshments	Fox House Inn, Longshaw Estate Café
Parking	Fox House Inn SK 267 802

This is a moorland walk full of archaeological and natural interest. Big Moor, now in the hands of a partnership of wildlife and nature agencies, is being developed with conservation and protection in mind. Those who delight in wildlife will find this walk especially fulfilling, with great diversity of birdlife, especially raptors, and a large herd of wild red deer to admire. In terms of archaeology, the area has stone circles, guide stoops, a stone cross and ancient ways. Lovers of Ordnance Survey ephemera have much to explore with triangulation pillars and hidden fundamental benchmarks making for a walk full of tick-features to collect.

Red deer are frequently seen on these moors, an incongruous sight when the city of Sheffield is the backdrop.

From Fox House Inn walk northeast along the **A6187** for 300 metres and cross the road to go through the gate then follow the wall line up the field and through a second gate leading onto a road. Cross the road and go through the gate opposite and follow the defined track to **Totley Moor**. Where a second road, coming from the right, joins the track, proceed for 270 metres then take the faint footpath on the right southeast up towards the skyline and the **triangulation pillar**. ◄

Head southwest to cross a tumbledown wall and carry on through the boggy ground of **Totley Moss** to reach a gate in a wall leading onto the **B6054**. Cross the

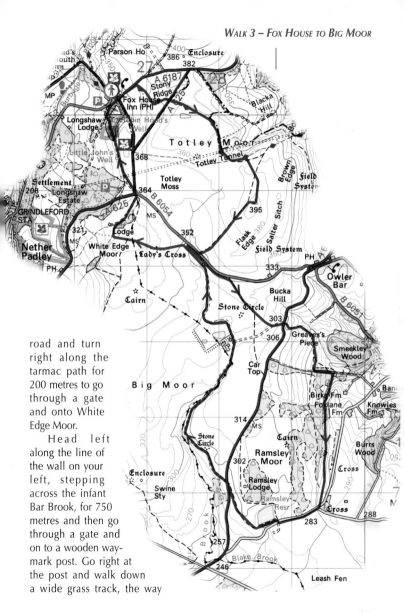

road and turn right along the tarmac path for 200 metres to go through a gate and onto White Edge Moor.

Head left along the line of the wall on your left, stepping across the infant Bar Brook, for 750 metres and then go through a gate and on to a wooden way-mark post. Go right at the post and walk down a wide grass track, the way marked by ancient trees on either side. At a fork in the track, keep left and descend the moor until the track intersects with a well-made vehicle track. Turn left along the track, passing an ancient guide stoop on the right, to a gate leading onto the **A621**. Go directly across and over a wooden stile to **Greaves's Piece** and along a grass footpath right, leading down into a valley.

> **Guide stoops** (stone guideposts) started appearing in the early 18th century to act as signposts on what had become trade routes across the moors. There are several examples on Big Moor; the one passed here indicates the way to Bakewell and Sheffield. Close to the guide stoop is a flat stone laid on the ground. This is a companion stone, part of an art project connected with the ancient ways around Big Moor.

Continue along the footpath to go over a wooden stile and into a fenced lane, known as Car Road. Turn left down the lane and take the next footpath on the right into woodland. Follow the footpath by the stream below Hewetts Bank, crossing it at a ford then rising above the valley and stream through a wooden gate to open moorland, joining a track that leads to a gate and a minor road. Go right along the road for 600 metres and take the footpath through a gate leading to **Ramsley Reservoir**. Turn left through the wooden gate and walk along the breached dam exiting via a gate onto a grass trail that turns northwest after 75 metres to arrive at a gate on the A621. Go straight across and through the gate opposite onto a wide footpath on **Big Moor**. Follow the path along to the **Stone Circle** just off to the right then regain the path and continue along this to reach a gate leading on to a house beyond.

> There is much evidence of **Bronze Age settlement** on the moor with several stone circles, cairns and field systems. The area was suitable for settlement having a good water supply from Bar Brook and fertile land in which to grow crops.

Lady's Cross on White Edge

Go to the right of the house and walk up to go through a gate then follow a footpath around a disused reservoir eventually reaching a second gate. ▶

Proceed through the gate along the footpath to return to Bar Brook. Cross the brook and turn left, ignoring the gate onto the road, but walk up the moorland path to pass **Lady's Cross** on the left and arrive at a wooden gate in a wall at White Edge. Go through the gate and down the steep footpath to **White Edge Lodge**. Turn right along the vehicle track to the road junction. Go across the road junction and enter the **Longshaw Estate** by the wooden gate at Wooden Pole. Take the wide grass trail down to join a second heading for **Longshaw Lodge**. At the lodge carry on along the exit drive from the estate but do not go onto the road. Instead take the footpath to the right up through trees to a gate leading to Fox House Inn and the end of the walk.

This is a good area to spot merlin, curlew, red start and skylark, among other birdlife; adders can also be seen basking on footpaths.

41

WALK 4

Fox House to Stanedge Pole

Start/Finish	Fox House Inn SK 267 802
Distance	16km (10 miles)
Ascent	335m
Time	5hrs
Terrain	Open moorland, footpaths and tracks
Map	OS 1:25000 Explorer OL1 Dark Peak
Refreshments	Fox House Inn, Longshaw Estate Café
Parking	Fox House Inn SK 267 802

There are no major ascents on this route, making it a restful walk through history with some wonderful views along the way. The Houndkirk Road and Long Causeway are both ancient trade routes linking Derbyshire and Yorkshire. Around the area are remnants of Second World War practice grounds and unusually the outline of a decoy town used to deflect bombers away from Sheffield. And finally there is Stanage Edge, with its new pole nearby, hidden caves, hundreds of climbing routes and spectacular views. This is a great walk that is easy on the feet.

Walk northeast from Fox House Inn for 400 metres along the **A6187**. Where the road bends right carry on left along the broad track of Houndkirk Road. Cross a track leading to Parson House Outdoor Pursuit Centre, go through the gate and proceed along Houndkirk Road.

Houndkirk Road was created in 1758 as a turnpike (toll) road from Sheffield to Tideswell and on to Buxton. The road has two milestones giving the distances to Tideswell and Buxton. Milestones became commonplace after 1709 and law by 1758, when local magistrates instructed that distance markers be placed every mile.

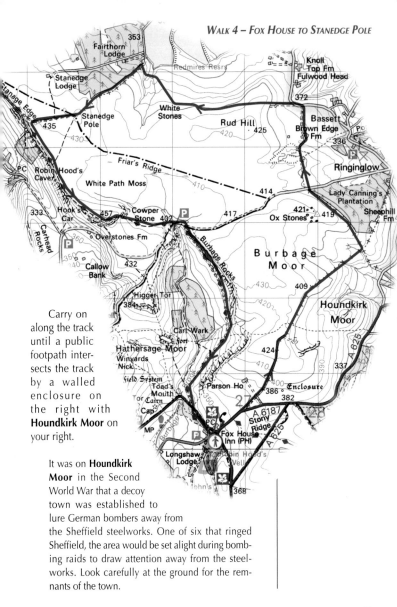

Carry on along the track until a public footpath intersects the track by a walled enclosure on the right with **Houndkirk Moor** on your right.

It was on **Houndkirk Moor** in the Second World War that a decoy town was established to lure German bombers away from the Sheffield steelworks. One of six that ringed Sheffield, the area would be set alight during bombing raids to draw attention away from the steelworks. Look carefully at the ground for the remnants of the town.

43

Shortly after, the track crosses Thieves Bridge spanning Redcar Brook and is crossed by a second track. Walk left up the new track, passing through a farm gate with **Lady Canning's Plantation** on your right. The route comes to a steel gate leading onto a road. Cross the road to the footpath directly opposite and continue over open moorland. Follow the footpath to just before a wall running almost east to west and turn left between two small hillocks to arrive at a stone stile crossing a wall at the far side of a farm gate. Cross the stile and go down the walled lane to a farm gate. Go through the gate and bear left between **farm buildings** to pick up the farm track leading to the road. At the road, go left to cross a ladder stile and walk along a permissive path, keeping a wall close on the left. Go through the right hand gate and up the field by the left hand wall to go through two wooden gates onto **Rud Hill**.

After a wooden stile the ground can be very boggy on this moor, so gaiters are advisable.

Cross the moor following the waymarked concessionary footpath, paying close attention to the small marker posts. ◄ The path drops down to a stile then a footbridge. Turn left onto the bridge and follow the path to a wooden squeeze stile leading onto a stone track.

The track is **Long Causeway**, a packhorse route that connected Sheffield and Hathersage and probably followed the Roman Batham Gate road for part of its course. The route was paved with stone, some of which can be seen as the Causeway rises up to Stanedge Pole.

Turn left and walk up Long Causeway passing through a gate and then along stone setts to reach **Stanedge Pole**.

Stanedge Pole sits at the side of Long Causeway. This current pole was erected in 2016 on the anniversary of the founding of the Peak National Park, as it was then called. From the pole's establishment in the 16th century its main use was as a boundary marker for the border between Derbyshire and Yorkshire and the ecclesiastical boundary of

The new Stanedge Pole

Canterbury and York. Dates and initials on the grit-stone around the pole denote the date a new pole was installed and the surveyor responsible. One quirk is the spelling on Ordnance Survey maps, which differs from the spelling of the gritstone edge that is nearby. Erroneously the metal casting holding the pole in place denotes Stanage Pole and not the correct Stanedge Pole.

From Stanedge Pole continue along Long Causeway walking over rutted stones set a cart width apart until you reach a waymark post and stone-flagged path leading left towards the gritstone edge. Follow this path to a stile on the left which, if crossed, would deposit you onto Stanage Edge. Go along the footpath passing Stanage Plantation and progressing to **Robin Hood's Cave**.

Stanage is the modern shortening of Stane Edge or Stone Edge. It is probably the most popular climbing crag in the country; the whole of Stanage Edge has over 1700 routes, most vertical in nature, making it a Mecca for generations of climbers. Robin Hood's Cave, a natural rock feature is a must to go

The caves on Stanage Edge

and see. After a bit of twisting and turning to gain entrance you are presented with a wonderful balcony from which to view the valley below.

Follow the footpath until you reach the triangulation pillar where the path turns left and starts its descent from the edge to the road ahead. At the road turn left and cross Upper Burbage Bridge, after which you should cross the road and enter the valley by the gate in front of the information board.

Burbage Rocks will be full of climbers, having many easier routes than Stanage Edge.

Take the wide footpath that runs below **Burbage Rocks** and follow this down through the valley, with Higger Tor and Carl Wark looming above on your right. ◀

The **footpath** was constructed as a shooting track for the Duke of Rutland to gain access to the grouse moors from his shooting lodge at Longshaw. The establishment of the shooting estate closed off

ancient roads across the moors and a remnant can
be seen towards the end of the track, to the right
in the valley below: a lonely packhorse bridge sits
astride Burbage Brook (the stream near the fortifica-
tion), below Carl Wark settlement.

Along the drive you will find large boulders
at the side of the track with strange indentations.
These were the result of rifle practice in the Second
World War.

At the end of the track go through the gate, straight
across the road to the gate in the wall and enter the
Longshaw Estate. Follow the woodland path and go
through the gate at the end to cross the road to the drive
leading to **Longshaw Lodge**. As soon as you have gone
through the drive entrance turn sharp left in front of the
gatehouse and walk up the footpath through the woodland, then through the gate in the wall, and cross the road
to **Fox House Inn**.

*Bullets holes on the
Burbage Gritstone*

WALK 5
Grindleford to Higger Tor

Start/Finish	Grindleford Station SK 251 787
Distance	10km (6 miles)
Ascent	342m
Time	3hrs
Terrain	Woodland paths and open moorland, gritstone edges
Map	OS 1:25000 Explorer OL1 Dark Peak, OS 1:25000 Explorer OL24 White Peak
Refreshments	Grindleford Station Café
Parking	Public road at Grindleford Station

The walk starts at Grindleford Station café, an institution in the Dark Peak. History is a constant feature of the walk. Almost immediately the walker reaches Padley Chapel, with its associations with the Reformation. Industrial archaeology is next as the walk follows the trail of stone that was used to build the Derwent Valley dams and comes across lines of millstones still waiting for collection. Leaving woodland the walk crosses moorland to Higger Tor before descending to Carl Wark, the site of an ancient settlement. The walk finishes by descending Padley Gorge with its tumbling waterfalls, back to Grindleford station.

Padley Chapel, Grindleford

From Grindleford station walk across the rail bridge and continue along the stone track, passing an old mill on the right to reach Padley Chapel. ▶

From the chapel continue along the track and go through a gate. Turn right immediately and follow the wall on your right up through Bolehill Wood. After 100 metres the footpath intersects another path at the wall corner; turn left here and proceed for 40 metres along a level path to the base of a steep incline.

When two priests were caught conducting a Catholic service here during the Reformation they were hung, drawn and quartered, becoming martyrs in the process.

You are in fact in the centre of the **incline**. Looking down to your left you can see a bridge; looking up to your right you can see a broad grassed incline with large boulders placed in the middle along its length. The incline was constructed to deliver stone cut from the quarries above down to a rail line below for transport to the dam constructions in the Upper Derwent Valley.

Ascend the incline, then at the top take time to recover before turning left to follow a well-defined sunken track north through woodland for 600 metres passing through a wooden gate. Stop at a second wooden gate in a wire sheep fence along with a walled enclosure on your left. Do not go through the gate but turn sharp right, doubling back and take the unmarked track heading southeast towards a narrow gap between two rock faces. Go through the gap then turn left through birch woodland to enter Bolehill

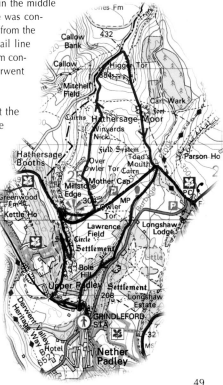

49

Millstones never collected from Bolehill Quarry

Look for the large stone water-trough, a remnant of the blacksmith's workshop.

Quarry. ◄ Regain the grass track and head north towards the road.

You will pass a great number of **millstones** on your right. These were made in the quarry and stacked for collection and delivery to customers. The millstones were used for grinding barley and oats and for crushing wood for pulp and paint manufacture. Imported millstones eventually became more commonplace and the production of Peak District millstones ceased. When the Peak National Park was established in 1951, the millstone was chosen as its emblem.

Go through the gate and turn right up the road. Just before the road bends left, cross and take the signposted footpath left for 30 metres, then sharp right on the footpath ascending between rocks to reach a low stone wall at **Surprise View vantage point**. Cross this wall and follow the track across moorland to the car park.

From the car park, take the gate that gives access to the moorland and follow the path northwards up towards the gritstone tors of **Mother Cap**, **Over Owler Tor** and **Winyards Nick**. From Winyards Nick the path gently descends towards a rectangular enclosure.

There are five such **enclosures** on the Longshaw Estate. They were built to protect black oats that were grown to feed the grouse on this shooting estate. Originally sheep grazed the moor but they proved to be a bar to the larger profits available from grouse, so the sheep were removed.

Turn left by the first wall corner and walk along the side of the enclosure to reach its opening. From here follow the track across moorland to skirt round the western edge of Higger Tor, keeping the road and sheep fence on your left. When you reach the gate at the top of the road, do not go through the gate but turn right and follow the stone steps up to attain the summit of **Higger Tor**.

Winter can arrive quickly in the Peak District, to the delight of some

Higger Tor is shaped like an arrowhead: go forwards to where the Tor forms the tip pointing south down across open moorland towards Carl Wark. Descend here and cross the moor to reach **Carl Wark**.

Carl Wark is thought to be the site of an Iron Age fort. There are signs of human activity: a wall that has been clearly manmade stands at the entrance to the fort. It is certainly in a prominent position with excellent views all round. The centre of the area is strewn with rock boulders, making the place difficult to settle, so it may not have been inhabited but used as a place of safety. There is a stone trough, carved out of a single boulder, that is evidence of more recent stone-working.

On reaching Carl Wark, go along the right edge to a stone trough then take the footpath south across the moor heading to the right of the sharp bend of the **A6187**. Near the road bear right to reach a gate and then go directly across the road and through a second gate to gain access to the **Longshaw Estate**.

Turn right and follow the footpath through Padley Gorge, keeping the stream nearby on your left. The footpath winds its way down through ancient woodland finishing at a gate that leads onto a track between houses. Go down this track and at the bottom turn left to retrace your steps to **Grindleford Station**.

CENTRAL DARK PEAK

The Dark Peak in all its glory (Walk 7)

The central area of the Dark Peak comprises shale, gritstone and peat. Atop this bedrock are ancient woodlands, Bronze Age settlements, industrial development and the cauldron of the outdoor movement that we have today. The landscape is often dark and brooding, occasionally wild. The weather will have a big influence on walks in these parts.

The moors are home to grouse, the mountain hare, golden plover, heather and peat. Peat means groughs: deep channels in the land that make a walk across a moor more challenging. It also means you need excellent navigational skills, particularly on Kinder Scout and Bleaklow.

The central Dark Peak has the most iconic of all gritstone edges – Stanage. Seemingly stretching forever down the Derwent Valley, it has rightly been a magnet for climbers over the decades and many of the routes were first climbed by some of the famous names of the sport.

Kinder Scout is where the Right to Roam movement took hold and the Mass Trespass of 1932 turned the tide in political and social thinking. Along with Bleaklow it provides some of the most memorable long walks across open moorlands in perfect quiet and solitude.

Head up the Derwent Valley to a different landscape of water and forest and gritstone edges looking down from above the valley floor. Popular with many, this is a valley of lost villages, wartime exploits and superb high-level walks.

WALK 6
Hathersage to Stanage Edge

Start/Finish	Hathersage bus shelter SK 230 815
Distance	8.5km (5 miles)
Ascent	330m
Time	3hrs
Terrain	Moorland footpaths and rocky terrain
Map	OS 1:25000 Explorer OL1 Dark Peak
Parking	Public car park, Oddfellows Road, SK 231 813

This walk starts in Hathersage, once a centre of nail production and later millstones for grain. It is now a centre of outdoor pursuits, and home to the excellent shop and café, Outside. The walk follows signposts across woodland and moorland to make an easy ascent of Long Causeway onto Stanage Edge. The views from here across the Dark Peak are suberb. From Stanage Edge the route descends to North Lees Hall, the inspiration for Mr Rochester's house in *Jane Eyre*, to Hathersage via the village church where you can see what is supposed to be the grave of Little John, the right hand man of Robin Hood.

From the bus shelter on Main Street in Hathersage take the road to the left, The Crofts, and follow the left hand pavement past a row of houses to reach a footpath leading to the cricket ground. Cross the ground keeping to the boundary with a stream on your left to gain a narrow footpath skirting a garden. Proceed along the path and on reaching allotments turn right and go through a gate that leads onto a track. Turn left along the track and continue along Baulk Lane across fields, passing through several field boundaries to reach **Brookfield Manor**.

Take the footpath to the right of the house to a road. Go straight across the road and through the gate and cross a field to a second gate into woodland. Enter the woodland and follow the footpath a short distance to reach a footbridge over a stream by a foot-path sign. Walk across the bridge and up through the woodland to a gate. Go through the gate and across the field to a second gate into another field. Enter the field and cross a wooden footbridge on the left then turn immediately right to arrive at a stile to the right of a house. Cross the stile onto a farm track and turn left to walk between houses and then, just past the house on the right, take the signposted footpath on the right. Go through the gate and ascend to cross a stile. With a wall on the right go through the gap in the wall then turn left to follow a footpath with the wall now on the left to reach a stone stile. Climb over the stile and, with **Dennis Knoll** on the left, continue onto the road. Turn right down the road and go through the first gate you reach in the wall on the left. Ascend the moorland to the **Buck Stone**, set in isolation in the middle of the moor.

The boulder, **Buck Stone**, has many handholds for the adventurous. It was also a favoured stopping point for the jaggers (a person who leads a team of packhorses) who used Long Causeway to take their packhorse trains across the county boundary.

From the Buck Stone continue on up through the moorland to reach Long Causeway.

This beautifully paved, ancient route leads to Stanage Edge. At the top is a rock carving depicting the road and its junction with the Long Causeway.

North Lees Hall, Thornfield Hall in Jane Eyre

The **Long Causeway** was once a major route for the transportation of goods from west to east. It was originally a paved track, marked on OS maps as a bridleway open to all traffic. Sadly the track was no match for modern four-wheel drive vehicles and it became necessary to close it to traffic in 2014 and apply protective surface coating.

Turn right up the track to reach the top of **Stanage Edge**. At the top go right for 50 metres then take the right hand footpath along the edge for 200 metres to reach a natural footpath that descends via stone steps down the face of the edge and on into Stanage Plantation. This is Golden Car Road. ◄

Follow the path through the woodland to a gate giving access onto a large clearing. Continue for 100 metres then take the left hand fork in the path to arrive at the road with a WC across the road on your right.

Go straight across the road and enter the woodland, then immediately left down through the trees to a track. Turn right along this track to go through a gate and take the left hand track down to **North Lees**.

North Lees Hall is a fine Elizabethan building of literary importance following visits by Charlotte Bronte in the mid 19th century. The author used the hall as the basis for Thornfield Hall in the novel *Jane Eyre*. In the book Mrs Rochester jumped to her death from the roof of the building.

Follow the footpath left along the front of the hall and descend the tarmac track to a road. Cross the road and go over a wall stile to reach a farm track. Turn right and follow the track for 50 metres then turn immediately left following a signed footpath to the left of the farm buildings. Continue along the footpath across fields to reach a small stream. Cross the stream and ascend the steps to go right to a gate leading onto a road. Proceed straight on from the gate with a **church** on the right. Ignore the first gate and go through the main entrance to enter the churchyard. Go left to visit what is reputed to be Little John's grave.

Little John was one of the outlaws commanded by Robin Hood. There was a Robin of Loxley, born in Loxley valley near Sheffield which is not far from Hathersage, so perhaps both Little John and Robin Hood did exist. Pay careful attention to the sign marking the 'grave', noting the length of the grave and the reputation of Little John.

From the main entrance carry straight on to exit the churchyard by a gate. Follow the footpath down with a very tall wall on your left and on reaching a gate go through it and then turn left to return to **Hathersage**.

WALK 7
Wyming Brook to Stanage Edge

Start/Finish	Redmires Reservoirs car park SK 256 856
Distance	18km (11 miles)
Ascent	530m
Time	6hrs
Terrain	Moorland footpaths and rocky terrain
Map	OS 1:25000 Explorer OL1 Dark Peak
Parking	Redmires Reservoirs car park SK 256 856

Wyming Brook is one of the most beautiful gorges within the Dark Peak. It has a strong, flowing brook tumbling over gritstone boulders; the noise after heavy rains can be deafening. The route meanders through towering Scots Pines teeming with wildlife, past the ancient Moscar Cross, along the old trans-Pennine road and then to Stanage Edge. The views across the Derwent Valley showcase the very best of the high moorlands encompassing Derwent: Bleaklow, Alport and Kinder Scout. The route also passes the unique Stanedge Pole, alongside the Long Causeway.

Leave **Redmires Reservoirs car park** at the northeast corner and turn immediately left into a walled lane. Pass through the gate, go up the hill and continue onto the moor keeping the wall on your right. Where the wall turns east carry straight on north across moorland descending a little to a stone bridge across a manmade water conduit. Cross the bridge and turn right along an elevated track. After passing a stone pillar on your right a gate blocks progress along the track.

The **stone pillar** is one of several used for sighting the course of a tunnel beneath the moor. It is the longest tunnel in England at 7km, with a fall of just two metres along its length. The tunnel delivers water from Howden Reservoir in the Upper Derwent Valley to a collection tank at the bottom of Wyming Brook. Due to seepage from the surrounding moor the tunnel delivers more water than it takes in at Bamford.

Turn left immediately before the gate and go through a wooden gate on your left to descend moorland to woodland, the top of which can be seen in the middle distance. On reaching the trees, step across a small

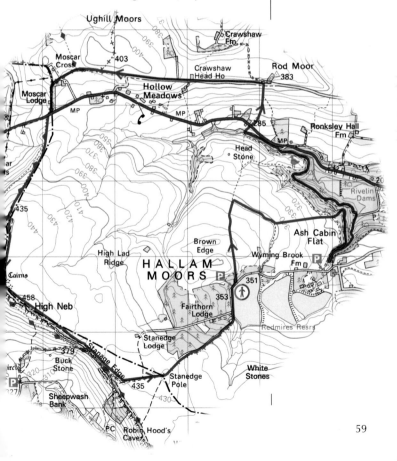

59

stream, noting the water-bowl carved into the gritstone on the ground, and go through the gate, walking straight on through the trees to reach a footpath heading to the right. Follow the path and after passing a wooden marker post descend through the trees to reach wooden steps down onto a wide forest track. Turn right and walk along the track until you reach a small car park. As soon as you enter the **car park** turn left and walk down to Wyming Brook flowing almost due north.

> **Wyming Brook** is looked after by a local wildlife trust and is part of a larger Site of Special Scientific Interest (SSSI). Originally the gorge was the private hunting grounds of the Lords of Sheffield Manor. Today the gorge teems with wild birds such as the dipper and crossbill, along with mosses, fungi and moths.

Cross the brook by the stepping stones and turn left at the signpost for **Rivelin Dams** to follow the brook down to a wooden bridge. Go across the bridge keeping on the path that switches over the brook several times down the

The tumbling Wyming Brook

60

Moscar Cross on the old Sheffield to Manchester road

length of the gorge. At the bottom go through the kissing gate then turn left on a bridleway for 2km until you reach a stone bridge across a stream flowing into the Rivelin Dams. Cross this bridge and turn left along a public footpath through trees, keeping the stream on your left.

top before a wooden footbridge over the stream and turn right up wooden steps to a stone stile leading into a field. Cross the field to a second stone stile leading onto the A57. Go right along the road for 10 metres and then cross to a wooden stile leading into a field. Go straight on across fields and stiles heading for the house with woodlands on its right on the horizon. Cross the final stile in front of the house onto the old Sheffield to Manchester road and, turning left, follow it for 2km until the road turns sharp left. Do not follow the road left, but carry straight on along a track, through two gates and a farm to arrive at **Moscar Cross**.

Moscar Cross marks the ancient crossroads of Sheffield, Hope, Bamford and Hathersage. The guide stoop dates from the early 18th century when it became law that each local authority had to place guide stoops at major access points. The original road at Moscar Cross turns to your right, indicated by Bradfield on the post. The old road can be clearly identified by the great width between the boundary walls, enough for a cart to pass. Note the levelling mark at the base of the guide stoop. Another can be found on a triangular-shaped rock at the side of the footpath to Stanage Edge.

Turn left at the cross and walk through gates down a wide tarmac drive to reach the **A57**. Turn right and then after 10 metres cross the road and go over the stile onto moorland. Follow the footpath up to **Stanage End** directly in front of you. Do not veer from the path. Eventually you arrive at a gap in a wall on the left with the remains of a quarry building on your right. Go left

Long Causeway heading for Stanedge Pole

here and up towards the edge turning right at the stone marker with the initials 'WW' to reach the footpath along **Stanage Edge**.

> **Stanage Edge** is Britain's most iconic climbing edge stretching for almost 5km from Stanage End to the Cowper Stone in the east. Along its length are hundreds of climbs and on any day rock climbers can be seen practising this demanding sport. This has not always been the case, as the edge and adjoining grouse moor used to be closed to the public and permission had to be sought from the landowner to gain access. Along the gritstone edge and upon the moor, 107 water-bowls have been carved, the purpose of which is said to be to collect rainwater for the grouse.

Continue along Stanage Edge, passing **High Neb triangulation pillar**, to eventually reach a wooden stile. Cross the stile and go straight on until the path meets a wide track coming up from your right, Long Causeway. Turn left up the track and follow this to reach **Stanedge Pole**.

> **Long Causeway** was used to transport goods from Hathersage and beyond across the moors and into South Yorkshire. Salt, lime, wool, lead and finished goods went one way while coal and iron came back into the area. The route was paved with gritstone slabs, still evident today on the approach to Stanedge Pole, however it has now been covered along most of its length for protection.

From Stanedge Pole follow the track left down to a gate, go through the gate and follow the track down to Redmires Reservoirs. At the road turn left and follow it to arrive back at the **Redmires Reservoir car park**.

WALK 8
Bamford Moor

Start/Finish	Heatherdene car park on the A6013 SK 202 858
Distance	12.5km (7½ miles)
Ascent	482m
Time	4hrs
Terrain	Open moorland and woodland
Map	OS 1:25000 Explorer OL1 Dark Peak
Refreshments	Yorkshire Bridge Inn, A6013
Parking	Heatherdene car park on the A6013 (opposite Ladybower Reservoir) SK 202 858

The walk starts with a steep ascent before heading across to a 400-year-old murder site and then onto Bamford Moor, which has archaeological and historical interest ranging from the Neolithic period to the 19th century. The moor was one of the last to see a mass trespass. However, although access is now available since the passing of the Countryside and Rights of Way Act 2000 (CRoW), restrictions still apply so it is always best to check online before setting off. The views from Bamford Edge at the end of the walk are spectacular and provide a fitting end to the day's walk.

From Heatherdene car park walk along the **A6013** to the **A57** and turn right to the **Ladybower Inn** car park. Cross the road and ascend the bridleway on the right of the pub, signposted 'Cutthroat Bridge' and 'Ashopton'. Walk up the track and take the footpath left signposted 'Ashopton'. Follow the path with a wall on the left to go through a gate and walk on until the trees are left behind and the road viaduct along the A6103 is directly to your left. Turn right here by a wooden pole and ascend the hillside up a wide track to **Ladybower Tor**, then on to the junction of a footpath and bridleway below **Whinstone Lee Tor**. ◀ From the junction, take the bridleway east towards **Highshaw Clough**. Where the bridleway meets another

There are superb views across the Upper Derwent Valley from the top of the Tor, so it is well worth the short ascent.

coming up
from Ladybower
Inn take the left hand
track down to go through
a gate and cross the A57 at
Cutthroat Bridge to cross a stile leading into woodland
directly opposite.

> **Cutthroat Bridge** got its name after a murder 400
> years ago when a man was found with his throat cut
> in Highshaw Clough and died some days later. The
> turnpike road from Sheffield to Manchester at that
> time followed the route you have just taken from
> Whinstone Lee Tor, but in later years was re-routed
> along its present day course and a bridge built near
> where the assault took place.

Go along the track through the woodland to emerge onto open moorland. Keep on the track below **Hordron Edge**. Follow the track as it turns sharp left, heading up a steep hillside with a stream to the right to emerge out onto open moorland with views of Stanage Edge beyond. Turn directly south and follow the track down into **Jarvis Clough**.

Do not cross the stream via the track but aim for the open shooting cabin further on. Walk in front of the cabin with the stream on your left for 40 metres to take a faint path leading up to grouse shooting butts. If you wish, at the third butt a compass reading can be taken, general direction southeast, to a cairn 100m away, the first of many to be passed on the moor. Retrace your steps to the butt and continue along their line until it ends. From here take a bearing, generally southsoutheast across a gently rising moor to the Glory Stones, a small boulder field with extensive views across to Win Hill. From the Glory Stones walk south to the high point clearly visible 450 metres away and explore the collection of **cairns** situated around this prominent area.

> The **cairns and enclosures** found on Bamford Moor form one of the most compact collections of Neolithic and Bronze Age habitation in the Dark Peak. Many of the cairns had a funereal purpose and may have contained more than one burial, indicating that they were of a ceremonial nature. Along with enclosures and hut circles they provide evidence of the settlements that existed on the moor from Neolithic through to Bronze Age and medieval times.

From the cairns walk east towards Stanage Edge on the horizon until you meet the remains of a wall running north. Cross the wall and continue in a general easterly direction for 500m to the stone monolith laid on the ground. From this menhir, known as 'The Old Woman Stone', take a bearing southeast to the **stone circle** 200 metres away, a superb example with clearly defined boundaries.

'The Old Woman Stone' was an ancient marker post or menhir for travellers crossing the moor. The stone is fluted from weathering when it stood upright. Standing at over two metres in height, it would have been one of the most imposing in the Peak District.

The Old Woman Stone

The **stone circle** sits on a small platform and is approximately eight metres in diameter. It is one of the most complete of all the small stone circles situated in the Peak District.

Leaving the stone circle, walk southwest towards a small wooded copse and a single standing stone. Turn right by the stone and descend through the copse to a fenced-in wood. Go right by the wood, keeping the fence on your left and walk down to cross a stream, then straight on across moorland to meet the footpath leading right to go along a quarry top in an anti-clockwise direction, until the quarry edge turns south. From this point follow the footpath northwest for 500 metres until the path forks.

Great Tor,
Bamford Edge

Take the left hand fork west, down through boulders to a rocky edge with Win Hill beyond. Turn right by a partially completed millstone and proceed along **Bamford Edge**. Stop at **Great Tor** to take in the magnificent views.

Continue along the edge path, to cross a tumble-down wall and then take the left hand path along the edge to a second wall. Continue for 20 metres and take the footpath heading downhill, eventually crossing a wall to enter a sunken lane down through ancient woodland to a wall bordering thick forest. Turn left and follow the wall downhill, keeping the wall and stream on your right. Go through a wall gap, then at an access point cross a stream, wall and stile into the forest, then turn left down the path and follow it to two sets of power lines situated in a wide clearing. Continue on the track as it curves left and descends back into woodland where a large stone pillar indicates the way right along a waymarked forest trail to return to **Heatherdene car park**.

WALK 9
Win Hill to Hope Cross

Start/Finish	Heatherdene car park on the A6013 SK 202 858
Distance	12.5km (7½ miles)
Ascent	430m
Time	4hrs
Terrain	A steep ascent on uneven ground to Win Hill then moorland, woodland and vehicle track
Map	OS 1:25000 Explorer OL1 Dark Peak
Refreshments	Yorkshire Bridge Inn, A6013
Parking	Heatherdene car park on the A6013 (opposite Ladybower Reservoir) SK202 858

The walk begins by crossing Ladybower Dam, with views along the Derwent Valley, then it is a steep ascent through woodland to Win Hill to enjoy panoramic views across the Dark Peak moors of Kinder Scout and Bleaklow and numerous valleys. The walk proceeds via the ancient Hope Cross to an abandoned farmhouse, set deep in the forest, then descends through the forest and along the reservoir track returning to Ladybower Dam. The challenge is to complete the Win Hill ascent at a consistent strong pace and without pause. It does not disappoint in its reward at the top.

From Heatherdene car park head due south along the Derwent Valley Heritage Way until reaching steps descending to the **A6013** on the right. Go down the steps and cross the road, then turn left along the footpath to reach **Ladybower Dam**. Turn right through the gate and walk along the dam. ▸

At the far end of the dam go through the gate, then straight on across the road and take the footpath opposite into woodland. Follow the path that gently ascends southsouthwest for 470 metres until it is intersected by a path rising steeply from the left at Parkin Clough. Turn right here and ascend Parkin Clough keeping the stream

The bellmouth overflow outlets on your right are known locally as 'the Plugholes' and are an impressive sight when the reservoir is overflowing.

The Great Ridge and Kinder Scout

on your left to reach a gate in a fence leading to open moorland. Go through the gate, turn right ten paces then immediately left at the finger post directing you to Win Hill. Walk up through the trees to follow first steps and then a track across open moorland to an opening in a drystone wall. Continue on through the wall opening for the final stage of the ascent of **Win Hill**.

Rest and take in one of the **finest views** in the Peak District. From here the Derwent Valley and Derwent Edge can be seen running from north to south. Bleaklow is on the northwest horizon, the Kinder Plateau to the west, Mam Tor and the Great Ridge in the south, and the long line of Stanage Edge to the east.

From Win Hill take the defined track west across moorland. Go through a field gate and continue along a grass track with a tree plantation on the right after 500

metres. Where the track eventually meets the tree plantation near **Wooler Knoll** at the junction of a drystone wall
and forest fence, go through the picket gate and continue
along a grass track bounded by a stone wall on the left
and a forest fence on the right. At the far end a picket gate
blocks the way. To the left is **Hope Cross**.

> **Hope Cross** is a two-metre-tall stone marker
> placed at the crossroads of four packhorse routes.
> Marked on the stone sitting on top of the pillar are
> four destinations along with the date 1737. Post
> and pillars were often used to mark routes across
> the Peak District before the days of turnpike roads;
> travellers used the routes for the transportation of
> goods and access.

Go through the picket gate and then
immediately right across a wooden
stile into the forest plantation
and continue along the gently descending
track until you
arrive at the

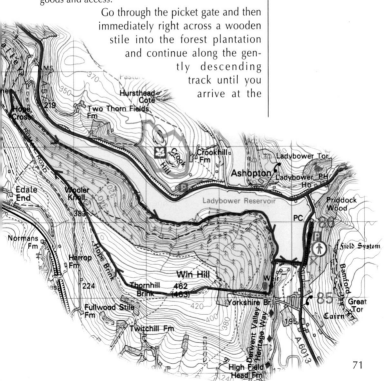

abandoned Elmin Pitts Farm. Walk across and to the left of the derelict buildings, now covered in mosses and being absorbed into the forest, and take the left hand track through a gap in a tumbledown wall to progress southeast among trees, eventually descending to a stone track with a gate to the left.

Turn right and walk along the track with the reservoir on your left until you reach Ladybower Dam. Turn left across the dam and retrace your steps to **Heatherdene car park**.

THE UPPER DERWENT VALLEY RESERVOIRS

Howden and Derwent dams were constructed in the early 20th century to supply water to Sheffield and cities in the midlands. A walk around Derwent Reservoir passes the remains of Birchinlee, a town built for the workers who built the dams. This was a major innovation for the workforce and came about partially due to the terrible living conditions that workers had to endure on previous constructions in the country.

Derwent Dam is famous as the practice dam for the Second World War Dambuster squadron of Lancaster Bombers. Before their mission to the dams in Germany's industrial heartland, the bomber crews practised their approach runs to drop the Barnes Wallis bouncing bomb. Each year a Lancaster Bomber flies over the dam in commemoration of the mission. The dam sits in a trench hundreds of feet deep with arms going into the hill at each side. This stops the dam from sliding down the valley. Books and pamphlets on the history can be found at the visitor centre.

Ladybower Reservoir was opened in 1945 and was the last of the three reservoirs to be created. It resulted in two villages being submerged: Ashopton village, the remains of which are beneath the Ashopton road viaduct carrying the A57, and Derwent Village, which was owned by the Duke of Norfolk. In times of drought or low water levels the submerged Derwent Village reappears at Mill Brook and it is possible to walk through the outlines of buildings and streets.

WALK 10

Kings Tree to Shepherds Meeting Stones

Start/Finish	Kings Tree, Upper Derwent Valley, SK 167 983
Distance	17km (10½ miles)
Ascent	540m
Time	5hrs
Terrain	Open moorland, gritstone edges and steep ascents
Map	OS 1:25000 Explorer OL1 Dark Peak
Parking	Public road SK 167 938. No access at weekends and Bank Holidays, except disabled. On summer weekends use the bus from Fairholmes SK 171 893.

This is a true Dark Peak experience. Wild and remote, and the landscape of the walk chooses its character with the weather. In summer the landscape is full of cottongrass and birdsong. In winter it can be deep in snow providing some of the best Dark Peak walking. The mountain hare is often seen on these moors but the best time of year to encounter it is in winter when it has its full white winter coat on. The walk starts at the furthest point of the road up the Upper Derwent Valley and quickly heads onto the high moorlands, before descending the Derwent Valley to climb up onto the Shepherds Meeting Stones. You then follow the edges along the top of the valley arriving at Crow Stone Edge before descending back into the valley to the start. It requires navigational skills and sturdy legs for the steep ascents. This is a magnificent walk at any time of year, but especially in winter.

From Kings Tree go through the gate leading up the valley and follow the reservoir track. Immediately after crossing a bridge turn left following the signpost up through woodland to **Linch Clough**. At the drystone wall go through the gate and continue along the clough for approximately 450 metres, keeping the stream on your left until you reach a tumbledown wall on the opposite bank. Choose a suitable crossing point to gain the opposite bank. Look to your right, upstream, to identify a grassed sledway rising up the **Cow Hey** first to your right, then after 50 metres turning left and ascending the hillside and disappearing out of view. Follow this line for 700 metres until you arrive at the remains of a wall pointing northwest up the moor. Follow the line of the wall until you reach a wide trench marked as Black Dike Drain on the 1:25000 OS map.

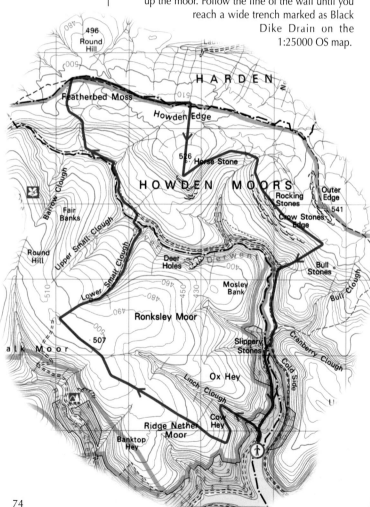

This wide **manmade channel** was originally thought to be a drain, used to channel water away from the moorland to enable sheep grazing to take place. In recent years further investigation has suggested that the channel was made by peat-cutting activities. The sledways (earthen ramps used to transport material up and down a hillside) that crisscross the hillside may support that view. The sled would be pulled along a sledway on a gentle gradient often running diagonally across the slope.

Continue along the channel until it forks. Take the right hand fork and walk on until the channel ends where it meets a track crossing it at right angles.

A **programme of work** has been carried out over recent years in this area to increase the land's capacity to hold water by stopping up the groughs (deep incised cuts in the peat layer) with dams to encourage new generation of peat. This has resulted in a wetter area and an increase in the diversity of plant and wildlife.

Turn right down **Lower Small Clough**, passing two shooting cabins, before reaching the **River Derwent**. Turn left and cross the river opposite Lands Clough to the opposite bank then turn left to follow the river upstream at times along a stone slab path. Where the river turns west, go right up Hoar Clough with the stream on your left. At the top scramble up a gritstone tor then head left across the clough to arrive at the Shepherds Meeting Stones.

From this point follow the path first west then curving north across moorland until you reach a path heading west to east at the highest point of the moor, the watershed between north and south. Go right and follow this faint path across **Howden Edge** keeping to the watershed line going east until you reach spot height 514m (marked on the 1:25000 OS map). Here turn right taking a bearing to reach Horse Stone Naze without encountering any

The Horse Stone near Horse Stone Naze

There is a way through but you have to work for it.

groughs. ◀ Naze is a corruption of nose and denotes a promontory or headland.

After Horse Stone Naze go northeast following the edge of the Naze to Stainery Clough Head. Cross the clough and on the opposite side turn south and walk to **Crow Stones Edge**.

Crow Stones Edge is a very typical gritstone outcrop formed some 300 million years ago when the area was a vast river delta. These outcrops are what are left of the gritstone cap as it was eroded and the valleys formed. The erosion often leaves rocks in a surprising balancing act and an excellent example, the Rocking Stone, can be found on Crow Edge.

From Crow Stones Edge follow the path southeast across heather moorland towards Broadhead Clough.

The remains of an **Airspeed Consul aircraft** can be found to the left of this path, just before reaching

Broadhead Clough, at grid reference SK 174 967 and on the 510m contour. The plane crashed in 1951 with the loss of the three men on board. There are many such sites in the Dark Peak. It is often an interesting navigation exercise to find them. If you do come across any of the crash sites please treat them with respect and do not remove any items.

On reaching Broadhead Clough descend right via the grouse butts to reach the River Derwent in the valley below.

Turn left and follow the track with the river on your right and then cross a small footbridge to reach **Slippery Stones bridge**. Cross the bridge and follow the vehicle track to arrive back at Kings Tree.

The bridge at **Slippery Stones** is the original pack-horse bridge from Derwent Village. Prior to the valley being flooded the bridge was removed and rebuilt at this location.

If the weather is sunny and the day has been hot, a few hundred metres upstream from Slippery Stones are some Fairie Pools. They are deep enough to languish in and experience the cool, soft peaty waters of the infant River Derwent.

WALK 11
Westend and Bleaklow Stones

Start/Finish	Westend, Upper Derwent Valley, SK 154 927
Distance	16.5km (10 miles)
Ascent	492m
Time	5hrs
Terrain	Open moorland, footpaths and tracks
Map	OS 1:25000 Explorer OL1 Dark Peak
Parking	Westend weekdays only, SK 154 927. No access at weekends and Bank Holidays, except disabled. On summer weekends use the bus from Fairholmes, SK 171 893.

This walk presents a wilderness experience in the Dark Peak: high moorland isolation, wide vistas and gritstone rock formations. From the River Westend, the walk quickly gains height to reach the moors above Alport Valley. It follows a series of natural rises in the landscape up onto Bleaklow, a nice test for any navigator. The high moors are currently undergoing huge changes under the Moors For The Future project. It is bringing a greater diversity in the wildlife and plants including golden plover, cottongrass, mosses, mountain hares and berries.

Here there are fine views across the Alport Valley onto Kinder Scout and the Great Ridge.

From the Westend bus stop take the left hand forest track into woodland. Where the track splits take the left hand track, signposted 'Ditch Clough', up through woodland to a gate leading out to open moorland. Go through the gate and follow the shooting track up, keeping Ditch Clough on your left. Eventually the track passes grouse butts before ending at **Birchin Hat**. ◄

With Alport Valley on the left walk along a footpath heading northwest until you reach two streams flowing down a clough. Cross the first stream and at the second cross and then head directly north for 90 metres rising up onto the moor, before again heading northwest across the

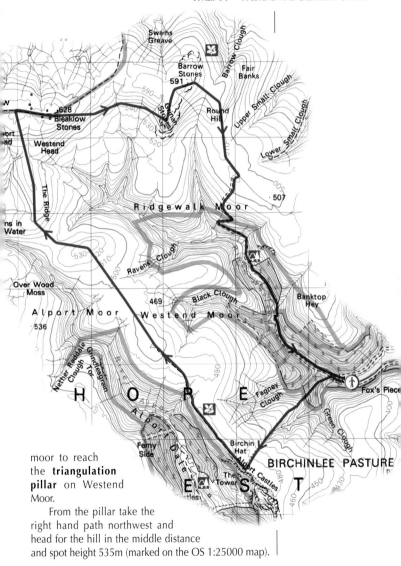

moor to reach
the **triangulation
pillar** on Westend
Moor.

From the pillar take the
right hand path northwest and
head for the hill in the middle distance
and spot height 535m (marked on the OS 1:25000 map).

The path descends slightly as it follows the crest of the watershed, before rising again to the spot height. Do not veer too much left or right or you will find yourself mired in peat groughs descending into the valleys below.

> The Dark Peak **groughs** are a feature unique to the Dark Peak. Made by the erosion of the peat, groughs are deep incisions in the moor, some as deep as six metres. They have a legendary status with Dark Peak walkers and there are many tales of boots being lost by people who have had to be pulled out of the cloying peat in the bottom of the grough.

Now walk west down the slope to reach the saddle between two cloughs falling left and right into the valleys below. From the saddle ascend the path rising northwest up **The Ridge** keeping on the ridgeline until you reach a fence. Take the left hand stile and follow the footpath up the hillside eventually turning right to reach Bleaklow

Heading out to the triangulation pillar above Alport Valley

*The Anvil at
Bleaklow Stones*

Stones seen on the horizon. From **Bleaklow Stones** take the footpath that descends southeast following the contours of the hillside, and ford several streams as the path works its way around Westend Head. Continue for 1700 metres, eventually rising to arrive at **Grinah Stones**. Take the path leading northeast away from Grinah Stones towards **Barrow Stones** aiming for its southern promontory and a gate leading onto Ridgewalk Moor below. ▶

Go through the gate and descend the path to **Round Hill**. At the cairn here turn right, south, and take the path across the moor to Black Dike Drain, and where a wide track crosses your path just past a moor pond, turn right and then immediately left at the grouse butt. Follow the track down the hillside passing through three gates to cross a bridge over the **River Westend**, then turn left following the forest track to the road and return to the start of the walk.

The gritstone shapes in this area have been left behind by erosion of the gritstone cap of the Dark Peak, and formed by the wind, rain and ice over millions of years.

WALK 12
Derwent Edge

Start/Finish	Fairholmes Visitor Centre SK 172 893
Distance	16km (10 miles)
Ascent	516m
Time	5hrs
Terrain	Road, footpath and track with some moorland walking
Map	OS 1:25000 Explorer OL1 Dark Peak
Refreshments	Fairholmes Visitor Centre SK 172 893
Parking	Fairholmes car park, located by the visitor centre, SK 172 893

Whatever your outdoor interest, whether it is birdwatching, geology, history or simply a good walk with superb views, this walk will not disappoint. It begins in the Upper Derwent Valley and follows a road through the remains of Derwent Village, before ascending to Derwent Edge, from where there are fine views along the Derwent Valley. There are numerous geological features of gritstone along the edge, weathered and worn into fantastic shapes over millions of years. The walk descends back into the valley via a hidden clough to the foot of Derwent Dam, where, if you are in luck, the water will be overflowing and cascading down the face of the dam. This walk has much to offer at any time of year.

From Fairholmes visitor centre head north towards Derwent Dam. Take care when walking down the road as it is always open to traffic. Continue on past Derwent Dam, the road curving right and becoming a narrow lane before it enters the remains of the settlement of **Derwent**.

Pass Mill Brook and proceed along the lane until two gates block the way ahead. Go through the left hand gate and up the meadow along a stone slab path. Go through the gate at the top to arrive at Grindle Barn. ◄ Carry on past the barn, through a gate and across a small ford to continue the ascent to Derwent Moors along a bridleway

This is a lovely place to sit and have coffee and admire the view of Win Hill and down the Derwent Valley.

track passing through four gates. At the fourth gate turn right along the bridleway and then take the left hand footpath, signposted to Moscar, which rises to the top of the

A gritstone waterbowl for the grouse

gritstone edge. Turn left at the top by the grouse butts and go northnortheast along a very well-defined path, passing the many rock features on either side, until you reach the triangulation pillar at **Back Tor**.

The **gritstone** was laid down between 360 million and 300 million years ago when the area was the outflow of a huge delta. Layers of sediment built up over millions of years and then erosion through wind and water carved out the valley leaving the harder sedimentary rock in place as edges and outcrops.

Some of the rock formations here are named after their shapes such as the Wheel Stones (or Coach and Horses), the Salt Cellar, Dove Stone and the Cakes of Bread. The edge also has several tors that look out over the valley. At the Ordnance Survey triangulation pillar on Back Tor, look for the strange rock carvings by the pillar.

From Back Tor head northwest along a stone footpath to **Lost Lad**, then descend stone steps towards the saddle. At the bottom of the steps take the shooting track on your right over open moorland and at the junction with a path coming from Lost Lad on your right, turn left and follow the track downhill towards Sheepfold Clough. ▶ Cross three stiles in sheep fences to arrive at **Abbey Brook** with Berristers Tor opposite.

Look out for the numerous waterfalls in the clough, especially after wet weather.

Welbeck Abbey were major landowners in this part of the Derwent Valley. Abbey Brook takes its name from this abbey as it had a grange (an outlying farm) situated within the clough. The monks of Welbeck Abbey employed tenant farmers to graze sheep in the area around the grange. The lands were taken away from Welbeck Abbey during the dissolution of the monasteries.

Bear left following the shooting track along the side of a hill until you reach a stile. Cross the stile and proceed straight on along the track crossing two fords before arriving at a picket gate by woodland. Go through the gate and follow the wall on your right to a second gate that gives access to a path down through woodland and brings you out onto the track that runs along the side of the **Derwent Reservoir**. Turn left and follow the track until you reach Derwent Dam. Go through the gate by the dam and descend the steps in front of the structure to retrace your steps back to **Fairholmes car park**.

WALK 13

Alport Castles and the Woodlands Valley

Start/Finish	Fairholmes Visitor Centre SK 172 893
Distance	12.5km (7½ miles)
Ascent	565m
Time	4hrs
Terrain	Open moorland, footpaths, tracks and steep descent
Map	OS 1:25000 Explorer OL1 Dark Peak
Refreshments	Fairholmes Visitor Centre SK 172 893
Parking	Fairholmes car park, located by the visitor centre, SK 172 893

Alport Castles is an unusual geological feature formed by a huge landslip. A Bronze Age barrow and a Second World War air crash site are located on the moor above. The crags looking down onto Alport Tower are home, in season, to peregrine falcons, and a hide is erected close by to allow people to view these magnificent birds. The hamlet of Alport is a typical, secluded settlement that interestingly has been the site of a 'Love Feast' for many years. The walk follows the river Ashop, which flows into both the Derwent and Ladybower Reservoirs by natural means and through human engineering. Crossing back over the Woodlands Valley the route descends through forest plantation passing another air crash site before returning to the start.

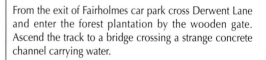

From the exit of Fairholmes car park cross Derwent Lane and enter the forest plantation by the wooden gate. Ascend the track to a bridge crossing a strange concrete channel carrying water.

> This **channel** is a conduit built to feed Derwent Reservoir with water from the River Ashop. The Derwent Valley Water Board had rights to all the water that flowed into the valley and this was one way of collecting water before Ladybower Reservoir was constructed.

Cross the bridge and take the footpath on the left to meet a wide stone track, go left and follow the track round a curve and up a small incline to take a footpath on the left signposted 'Lockerbrook'. The path leads up steps to a wooden gate leading into a field. Cross the field and go through a second gate onto a track. Turn left along the track, passing Lockerbrook Outdoor Centre on your left, until you reach the junction of paths and bridleway at the edge of a wood.

Do not descend to Hagg Farm but take the farm track immediately on your right to a wall with a gate and ladder stile leading to Bellhag Tor. Go over the stile and across the pasture to cross over the stile at the end and bear left by the corner of the wall, following the footpath, which eventually becomes stone-flagged in sections. ▶ Keep on the path until you reach **Alport Castles** ahead on your left.

When you reach spot height 483m, turn right and navigate to SK 152 905; in this vicinity you will find the remains of a Boulton Paul Defiant airplane that crashed in 1941.

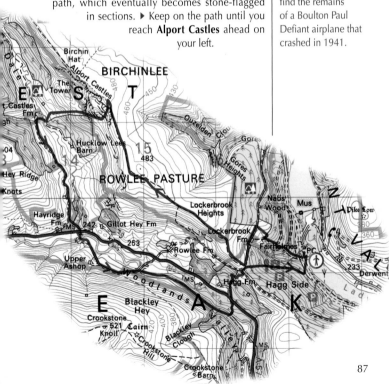

Alport Castles is an interesting geological site. The carboniferous rock was subject to a slide and flow failure, the vertical escarpment sliding away from the landmass above Alport Tower (which remained largely intact) then flowing out across the valley floor. This site is one of only a few in the UK where an event of this significance occurred.

In the summer months a bird hide is situated here to watch a pair of peregrine falcons who, for several years, have nested on the rock face.

Just after where the wall descends to Alport Castles take the faint footpath left down to a wall junction and pass between two stone gateposts. Follow the footpath down with the wall on your right around Little Moor. Cross a stile and now with the wall on your left continue descending to a second stile. Go over this stile and walk downhill to a wire fence, first on the right then left as the footpath progresses to the valley floor. At the bottom turn left by the **River Alport** and then cross the bridge. At the

The Tower at Alport Castles

other end of the bridge turn right then immediately left up a small hill to go over a stile and across a small field to a gate in the left hand corner to arrive at Alport Hamlet.

> **Alport** was recorded in the 14th century, and the farms and the hamlet date from the 17th century. It is one of the few inhabited valleys in the Peak District without traffic. It is also the place where the annual religious 'Love Feast' festival is held, on the first Sunday in July.

HANNAH MITCHELL

The socialist and suffragette Hannah Mitchell was born in Alport in 1871. Born into a poor farming family, her early years were hard, dominated by toil, an unhappy relationship with her mother, and a lack of schooling. Her father, however, taught her to read and she devoured everything she could. The two highlights of her year, the Hope hiring fair and the annual Love Feast, were not enough to keep Hannah Mitchell in Alport. At the age of 14 she left and recounts leaving the hamlet and walking across the moorland road to Manchester in tears. Hannah became involved in the new socialist movements that were springing up in the latter part of the 19th century and emerged as a well-known speaker on women's rights, eventually becoming a councillor and magistrate. She wrote a book on her life, *The Hard Way Up*, which was found among her belongings and published after her death. It has become one of the cornerstones of women's suffrage literature.

Go through the gate and left out of the farmyard passing through a second gate and continue along a farm track for 1.5km then follow a signpost pointing left across a small field. Go over two stiles at the bottom of the field to reach the A57 via a wooden gate. Cross the road and go through the gate opposite to ford the river. ▸

Note the football pitch on the opposite bank, a strange sight in this landscape.

Take the middle of three tracks rising along a sunken lane to a gate giving access to **Blackley Hey**. Walk along the track until it splits in two. Take the left hand track signposted 'Upper Derwent' down towards Rowlee Bridge. After crossing the water conduit turn right and follow the footpath alongside it, passing through woodland

The ancient Woodlands Valley

and three gates to reach a round stone structure. Take the footpath left over the stream and continue through the forest to reach a track. Turn left and cross the bridge to rise up and cross the **A57**, and then follow the steep tarmac lane directly opposite to a gate near **Hagg Farm**. Go through the gate and up a stone track through a second gate to arrive back at the footpath and bridleway junction encountered earlier in the walk.

By the stone post, go over the stile on your right, signposted 'Fairholmes', which leads into woodland, and follow the path down through the forest. Where the path goes through a wall, go left after the wall for 20 metres to find the site of a Meteor Jet that crashed in 1950 and then retrace your steps. Continue down the woodland path until you reach a short post indicating a footpath down to the left. Follow this down to the road then turn left to arrive back at **Fairholmes visitor centre**.

WALK 14
Margery Hill to Back Tor

Start/Finish	Fairholmes Visitor Centre SK 172 893
Distance	21km (13 miles)
Ascent	576m
Time	7hrs
Terrain	Open moorland, footpaths and tracks
Map	OS 1:25000 Explorer OL1 Dark Peak
Refreshments	Fairholmes Visitor Centre SK 172 893
Parking	Fairholmes car park, located by the visitor centre, SK 172 893

This particular route offers a good day's walking. It explores some of the less frequented cloughs and more secluded parts of the valley, with wonderful surprises along the way in the shape of waterfalls, wildflowers, mosses, lichens and small mammals. Good navigation is required as paths can be indistinct and – dependent on the management of heather – it is not unusual for paths to disappear completely. The views from the triangulation points and the edges are expansive with most of the central Dark Peak laid out before you.

From Fairholmes Visitor Centre take the footpath that leads down the road then carry on to Derwent Dam. Walk across the field at the foot of the dam and up the steps in front of the east tower. Turn left past the tower gatehouse and through a gate leading onto the east track heading north with **Derwent Reservoir** on your left.

Follow the eastern track for 4km and after passing Howden Dam take the footpath right, signposted 'Howden Clough', up through trees to a gate leading onto the moorland. Go through the gate and cross the stream on your left to start the ascent of **Howden Clough**. Keep to the faint footpath that curves around the hillside above the clough, eventually levelling out by a line of

The beautiful Howden Clough

grouse butts running east to west towards Howden Edge. Carry straight on north across **Upper Hey** to the top of **Cranberry Clough**.

Where the stream enters the clough go east for 100 metres then north again to cross the stream leading into Little Cranberry Clough. Turn northeast and follow the stream uphill until you meet the faint path running north below Wilfrey Edge. Turn left and proceed along this path until you reach a stile in a sheep fence; cross here and walk straight on to meet the Cut Gate bridleway rising up from the Upper Derwent Valley. Turn right and walk up the bridleway to a large cairn at the summit. Take the footpath southeast across open moorland, crossing a wooden stile to gain access to **Margery Hill** and its triangulation pillar.

From the triangulation pillar walk southwest for 150 metres to pick up the edge path and follow this generally south for 1.8km. Before the path starts its steep descent onto Nether Hey turn left by the anvil-shaped gritstone

towards Wet Stones and descend gently southeast, initially along a shooting track and then across the open moorland of Robin Hood Moss for 1.2km. Turn west across the moor to reach Cartledge Brook and cross to the opposite bank then follow it downstream until the brook turns right just after the junction with a stream coming in from the left. Follow the footpath northeast up to meet Dukes Road at a stone pillar.

Go right along Dukes Road towards Back Tor high on the skyline, the paths alternating between peat and stone flags. At **Back Tor** enjoy the view then go south along stone flags for 250 metres to the tall boundary stone on the left of the path. Turn west here and walk down through heather moorland, the path curving round first right and then left at **Green Sitches**. Where the path joins with the track coming from Lost Lad bear left and at the next path junction left again across open moorland to a signpost pointing left to Ladybower.

Follow the track to a wall just after a footpath sign and turn right across the moor to a stile in a fence. Go over the stile, then straight on down a wide sunken track with views of Derwent Dam on your left. Follow the track down to just before the start of the tree plantation and take the right hand path down to a wall. Follow the wall right then go left through a wooden gate in the wall to descend a steep hillside to a second gate that leads onto a tarmac roadway. Turn left along the road and at the next road junction go sharp right following the road beneath Derwent Dam to return to **Fairholmes Visitor Centre**.

WALK 15
Low Bradfield and Dale Dyke

Start/Finish	Low Bradfield car park SK 262 920
Distance	10km (6 miles)
Ascent	372m
Time	3hrs
Terrain	Footpaths and tracks
Map	OS 1:25000 Explorer OL1 Dark Peak
Refreshments	Low Bradfield, High Bradfield
Parking	Public car park SK 262 920

This is a Sunday afternoon type walk, with lots of history to explore at a gentle pace. The walk starts in Low Bradfield ascending through the fields to High Bradfield with its superb church and Norman motte and bailey. Further along there is a vantage point from which you can observe the birds that inhabit the rocks and woodlands before dropping down to Dale Dyke Reservoir, the scene of one of the worst civilian disasters in British history when the dam burst killing hundreds of people. The walk finishes back in Low Bradfield where, on a Sunday, a traditional scene of English village cricket can be enjoyed.

From the car park in Low Bradfield turn right down the walled lane in a northeasterly direction to cross a bridge over a stream and turn left along a lane to steps on your right. Ascend the steps and at the top turn left then immediately right up a narrow lane with a wooden fence. At the road go straight across and through an iron gate then cross the small field to go over a wooden stile and up a sunken lane with trees on the right, to open fields. Keep walking by the left hand wall to cross a second field with the wall now on your right, heading for the church. Go through the gateway and along a raised footpath to reach a wrought iron gate into the churchyard at **High Bradfield**.

High Bradfield Church

A **church** has stood on this site since Norman times. The present church was remodelled during the 15th century in Gothic style. Inside the church stands an original ninth-century Saxon Cross. There is also a memorial to the victims of the Great Sheffield Flood caused by the failure of the Dale Dyke Dam nearby. In the churchyard is the grave of William Horsfield, who found the crack in the dam and alerted workmen.

Facing the church door go left to the corner of the church and up the path turning left at the top by the wall and continue through the churchyard, passing through two gates and a gap in a stone wall at the end to enter woodland. ◄ Bear right following a signpost along a footpath above a steep, wooded hillside to your left, until a fence ahead blocks the way. Walk left between two stone gateposts then down the hillside to a gate. Go through the gate and cross the stream via a footbridge, then turn left and follow the track round to the right.

Immediately sharp right is the entrance to the motte and bailey castle.

Pass a ladder stile on the left and go on until you come to a gate on your left leading into a forest. Turn

96

right here and ascend a small knoll to a gap in the wall on the left. Continue through the gap and follow a grass farm track to the right of trees. When you arrive at a short length of wall go over the stile and turn right across the field to go over a ladder stile situated in a gap in the trees. Head left and follow the treeline to walk past farm ruins at Rocher Head and up the farm track crossing three stiles to reach a road.

The area around this road junction is often a very good place to view **raptor birds** soaring above. The woodlands and reservoir fringes are also excellent for spotting a variety of woodland birds including spotted flycatchers, dippers, woodpeckers, tree creepers, meadow pipits, curlew and a whole host of other interesting birds.

Go left then immediately right and walk down the road to the first footpath on the left. Pass through a gate and along a footpath, with a wall on the left, through a further gate and over a wooden stile to descend through woodland to a track at the side of **Agden Reservoir**.

97

Turn right along the reservoir track and continue to cross a stone bridge over a stream, then follow the track up through woodland and pass through stone gateposts by a wooden seat. Bear right into woodland following the track left over a stone bridge then onto a road on Wilkin Hill. Go right along the road to a junction and turn left here and take the first public bridleway on the left down to a stile. Go over the stile and down the track with a stone wall on your right then through a farm gate onto a road. Cross the road and take the footpath leading to Dale Dike Reservoir.

A **small stone** with the initials CLOB marks the Centre Line of the Old Bank where the dam used to be situated. One night in 1864 the dam burst sending millions of gallons of water down the Loxley Valley, killing 244 people. There is an information board giving more detail.

Walk along the track and where the track forks take the left hand path down to a footbridge across the outlet below the dam. Go across the bridge; turn right past the reservoir outlet to ascend stone steps on the left through woodland. Walk along with **Dale Dike Reservoir** on your right, past a stone building and take the footpath signposted left over a stone stile in the wall. Ascend through woodland on the footpath and turn left where the path meets a crossing track to reach Blindside Lane where the path leaves the woodland. Turn left down the lane and where it bends sharp left go over a wall stile on the right and bear right across fields to turn left into Mill Lee Road and back into **Low Bradfield**.

WALK 16
Langsett to Howden Edge

Start/Finish	Langsett Barn SE 211 004
Distance	15.5km (10 miles)
Ascent	501m
Time	5hrs
Terrain	Open moorland, footpaths and tracks
Map	OS 1:25000 Explorer OL1 Dark Peak
Refreshments	Langsett
Parking	Langsett Barn SE 211 004

Cut Gate from Langsett to Derwent was originally used for travelling from the market towns of South Yorkshire into Derbyshire. The track is an easy one to follow, but on reaching Howden Edge the walk requires good navigation. Howden Moor is typical Dark Peak moorland: wonderful in summer, but in winter and in poor visibility the moors require a high degree of skill to navigate. It is less frequented these days but still has a reputation for deep peat bogs; many is the walker who has struggled to extricate him or herself from the black ooze.

From Langsett Barn car park take the western footpath exit through a gap in a wall and into woodland. Follow the central woodland path through the trees keeping **Langsett Reservoir** on your left and at the next fork in the path keep left. At the footpath junction bear right along the reservoir side to reach a wide stone track. Follow the track down and cross the bridge keeping left to go through the left hand gate. The area to the left was a tank target practice ground and is worthy of exploration; see the box in Walk 17 for further information.

Continue along **Cut Gate bridleway** generally south then southwest rising gently for 5.5km. ▶ The route passes a footpath sign for Hazelhead, runs along Mickleden Edge and crosses several fords before arriving

Gate comes from the Norse for street. Cut may well be a derivation of cart.

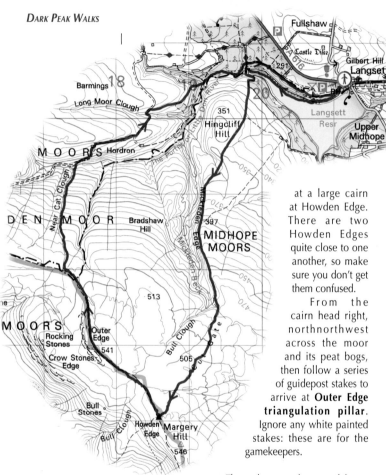

at a large cairn at Howden Edge. There are two Howden Edges quite close to one another, so make sure you don't get them confused.

From the cairn head right, northnorthwest across the moor and its peat bogs, then follow a series of guidepost stakes to arrive at **Outer Edge triangulation pillar**. Ignore any white painted stakes: these are for the gamekeepers.

The path across the moor follows the **watershed** between the River Derwent, which flows into the Trent, and the River Don. The Don originally flowed into the Trent at Hatfield. During the 17th century the area around the Hatfield Levels was drained for agricultural land and the Don was diverted to enter the River Ouse near Goole.

From the triangulation pillar the next leg continues for 1.2km. Keep on the path, generally north, until parallel with Outer Edge on the left and Harden Grough on the right. From here follow a faint path to the left of Harden Grough, coming to boundary stones with the letter 'B' chiselled on the face, the stone on the left having the letter reversed.

These **boundary stones** mark the various grouse shoots laid out across the Dark Peak moors. The initials generally denote the owner of the shoot and not necessarily the landowner. Later on in the walk you will pass the grouse butts where the guns are stationed.

After crossing several small groughs that lie on a general north–south line, you will arrive at the second of two thick wooden posts, with stones at its base, where the path takes a western heading. Walk north from the wooden post to proceed down **Near Cat Clough** keeping the stream on your left.

The boundary stones near Harden Grough

Pass a series of grouse butts on the left before descending to the Little Don River. Go over the bridge and ascend the hillside opposite to a large walled enclosure and stone cabin. Follow the track round to the right of the enclosure and go right by the corner of a wall that is on a west–east line and proceed along the track, keeping the wall on your right at all times.

At the stone guide stoop follow the track left down to a ford in the middle of an 'S' bend then, just after where the wall on the right ends at a large stone pillar, go right and continue along a grass track, unmarked on map, towards the trees of the Swinden Plantation until a fence blocks further progress. Go right at the fence and down the hillside to a stream with a single stone across it. Cross the stream here and go on to a gap in the wall ahead. Go right, through the gap in the wall and follow the footpath up through the trees, keeping the wall on your right and the fence on the left. Follow the edge of the plantation with river and slope on your right until you reach stone steps. Go down the steps to the river below and follow the fence on your left to reach a wooden gate.

Go through this gate and ascend stone steps. At the top turn right and follow the footpath through woodland with a stream on the right to reach a path junction by a waterfall. Turn right across the wooden bridge and go uphill, and then cross a concrete track to gain a woodland footpath to return to **Langsett**.

WALK 17

Langsett to Pike Lowe

Start/Finish	Langsett Barn SE 211 004
Distance	11km (7 miles)
Ascent	382m
Time	4hrs
Terrain	Open moorland, footpaths and tracks
Map	OS 1:25000 Explorer OL1 Dark Peak
Refreshments	Langsett
Parking	Langsett Barn SE 211 004

This is a delightful short walk full of wonderful scenery and commanding views across Yorkshire. It is also rich in Second World War history. The moors were used for tank target practice as well as the usual ground troop exercises, and consequently there is still a great deal of ordnance to be found. The views from Pike Lowe across Yorkshire are the high point of the walk, and the walk also provides the opportunity for some navigation practice before venturing out on some of the longer moorland walks.

From Langsett Barn car park take the western footpath exit through a gap in a wall and enter into woodland. Follow the central woodland path through the trees keeping the **Langsett Reservoir** on your left and at the next fork in the path keep left. At the next footpath junction bear right along the reservoir side to reach a wide stone track leading down to a bridge. Cross the bridge and go through the left hand gate onto **Cut Gate**. This ancient track leading across the moors, joining Yorkshire with Derbyshire and Cheshire, was an important trading route especially for salt from Cheshire and livestock being taken to market at Penistone from Derbyshire.

Continue up Cut Gate for 3.5km until the track, paved with stone, crosses a small ford. Where the track starts to ascend the hillside beyond the ford turn left, east,

Ancient field boundary

onto the moor to reach Lost Lad. This is a different Lost Lad to the one mentioned on Walk 14. From the spot height on Lost Lad walk across Sugden Top on a general eastern heading to reach **Pike Lowe** which is clearly visible on the horizon.

The site of the Bronze Age burial mound of **Pike Lowe** was most likely chosen because it is the highest point on Midhope Moors. Pike means Peak and Lowe or Low comes from the Old English 'hlaw' meaning burial place. The burial mounds in the Dark Peak have the remains of the cremated in vessels sealed with flat stones. The cairn on Pike Lowe is a much later addition and is continually being added to.

This is one of the disused tank targets constructed for training in the Second World War. A second is sited on the opposite side of the Sugden Clough.

From Pike Lowe head directly north down the moor, keeping the stream to your left until you come to an oddly placed brick-and-concrete structure running almost east–west. ◄

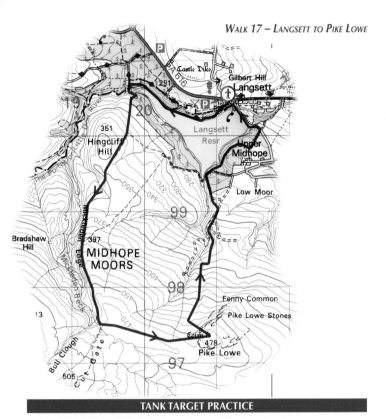

TANK TARGET PRACTICE

The moors around Langsett were an important training ground for troops in the Second World War. Langsett Reservoir was protected by a series of nets stretched across the reservoir to stop torpedoes from destroying the dam and thus stopping steel production further down the valley. You will notice concrete roads on the moor. These were made from the rubble caused by bombing in the Sheffield Blitz, and used for transporting tanks and materials up to the target ranges. The remains of North America Farm are all that is left of the farm buildings after they became a target for tank exercises. Tank tracks are still evident. If you come across any ordnance – often it is revealed after heavy rains wash away the peat – please do not touch it, but establish its position and report it to the Ranger Centre at Langsett Barn.

World War Two Tank practice target

The route now crosses the moor in a zig zag pattern crossing one stream and heading for the well-defined track going around the hillside below Range Moor Top directly ahead. On reaching this grass track follow it until it meets a shooting track coming up from the Sugden Clough below and running to your right around the hillside, eventually joining the concrete roads (see box). Head left down the road until you come to a waymark post pointing down left. Follow this path to a forest plantation and then take the footpath between the wall and the forest down to a wooden gate and exit onto a broad track at the side of the reservoir. Go straight across the track and take the woodland footpath opposite along the edge of the reservoir, following the waymark signs to a track running between the woodland and a wall. Turn left down the track and at the road junction turn left again following the road across the dam to the junction with the **A616**. Turn left, then left again to follow the footpath signs through the tiny hamlet of **Langsett** to return to the car park.

WALK 18
Torside to Bleaklow Head

Start/Finish	Torside car park SK 068 983
Distance	16.5km (10 miles)
Ascent	563m
Time	6hrs
Terrain	Open moorland, footpaths and tracks
Map	OS 1:25000 Explorer OL1 Dark Peak
Parking	Public pay and display car park SK 068 983

Bleaklow towers above the Longdendale Valley, giving a brooding impression on a cold winter's day. The walk follows the Pennine Way up to Bleaklow Head, with extensive views across the whole of the Dark Peak and on to the Pennines. Gritstone outcrops have been worn into fantastical shapes and time is well spent exploring these around Bleaklow Head. The route across the moor to Near Black Clough requires good map and compass work and should only be undertaken by experienced navigators. The main feature of this walk is the sense of wilderness and quiet.

Leave the Torside car park via the footpath and gate leading to the Longdendale Trail. ▶ Turn right along the trail and continue through two gates to reach a road. Do not cross the road but take the farm track on your immediate left across a cattle grid and follow the signposts for the Pennine Way and Bleaklow Head. Before reaching the farmhouse at **Reaps**, take the footpath right, signposted 'Pennine Way', up a grass hillside, through a tumbledown wall and then onto a stone-flagged path to reach a gate with the acorn sign on the gatepost indicating that you are on a National Trail.

This is a former rail line that has been converted for walkers and cyclists.

Bleaklow marks the end of the first day's walking on the **Pennine Way**. Walkers descend Torside and work their way across to the campsite at Crowden.

It is a navigational challenge from Edale to cross Kinder Scout and then Bleaklow and arrive before nightfall. But worse is to come the next day as walkers face the peat bog hell of Black Hill. A traumatic first two days in anyone's book.

Go through the gate and ascend the footpath, which rises steeply before levelling out to skirt the right hand side of **Torside Clough**. Eventually the path meets with stone flags at a stile. Cross the stile and continue the gentle ascent, passing a grouse butt on your left. This is known as the Pulpit due to its elevated position above the clough.

Keep on the rising path until you reach the junction of two cloughs below you with a small post showing the acorn sign and an

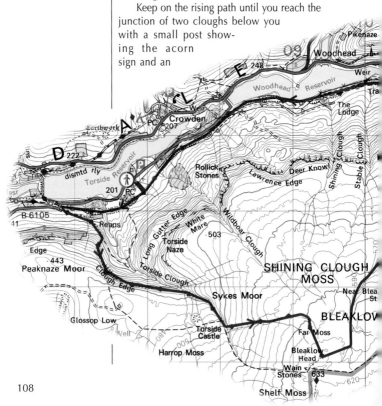

Bleaklow Head Cairn

arrow pointing down from the path to the confluence of the two streams below. A broad clough heading east faces you and this is the objective. Descend to the streams and ford the stream to the right and then the stream to the left to attain Wildboar Grain. Turn right and follow the stream on the right upwards to the skyline. ▶

Wildboar Grain is a branch tributary, the word grain meaning branch (several branches are known as grainings).

The path continues east before heading due south after 1.2km to arrive at a large cairn with a pole in the centre. This is **Bleaklow Head** and the highest point of the walk.

Bleaklow Head is the second highest point in the Peak District after Kinder Scout, its close neighbour. The name conjures up a Dickensian image of a harsh landscape with little merit. It can certainly be harsh, and no one should venture up it unprepared, but it can also be very beautiful at any time of year. In winter it is almost Narnian, and in summer the cottongrass and birdlife are abundant.

From the cairn take the path eastnortheast for 450 metres to reach the footpath that descends Near Black Clough. The route crosses many groughs, deep incisions in the peat that can be confusing to the navigator, and the path is also indistinct in places with no markers, so good navigation and concentration is required. After 450 metres a small stream is reached heading north down Near Black Clough. Follow the stream, crossing occasionally, but finally with the stream on your right hand side, passing through a broken wire fence with wooden poles to enter the steep sided **Near Black Clough**.

Follow the footpath down which eventually descends right through trees to a well-made vehicle track at the side of a wide stream. Turn left along the track and follow this down keeping the stream on your right to a gate.

Go through the gate and turn right and once over the bridge turn left between wooden rail fences and onto the remains of a rail platform for the defunct Woodhead Station. Continue along the Longdendale Trail to arrive back at **Torside car park**.

WALK 19
Wildboar Clough to Lawrence Edge

Start/Finish	Torside car park SK 068 983
Distance	9.5km (6 miles)
Ascent	493m
Time	4hrs
Terrain	Steep rocky scramble, footpath and open moorland
Map	OS 1:25000 Explorer OL1 Dark Peak
Parking	Public pay and display car park SK 068 983

When the chance comes to add a frisson of excitement to a walk it would be remiss to leave out Wildboar Clough. It has been hewn out of the crag face by waterfalls that provide a thundering soundtrack to the day's outing. The walk is best attempted after a period of dry weather to allow the slippery rocks chance to dry. Do not attempt the walk if you are unsure or unprepared. In winter the waterfalls can freeze and unless you are skilled in the use of axe and crampons the route is best avoided. In good conditions the day will not be forgotten.

Exit the Torside car park onto the Longdendale Trail and turn left heading northeast for 220 metres to a signpost on the right pointing the way to Wildboar Clough. Follow the directions up steps and over a stile to cross moorland sparsely planted with trees to a second stile in a wire fence. Go over the stile and turn right to follow the footpath, keeping the wire fence on your right. At a stone wall cross into woodland and follow the path up through ancient trees to emerge at a stile in a fence with the steep sides of **White Mare** beyond. The path works its way around the steep face and starts to gradually feed you down into the boulder-strewn floor of **Wildboar Clough**.

The peat of Bleaklow sits atop the **millstone grit** of the Carboniferous Period that in turn sits above shale. The millstone grit was formed from the out-flow of a huge river delta over 300 million years ago. Water coming off the Bleaklow Plateau cut through the peat covering and started its erosion of the millstone grit, hence the many cloughs that descend from the plateau to the valley floor. Wildboar Clough is one of the newest as the rock is still prominent across the incision. Older cloughs are deeper with a narrow stream along the bottom bounded by steep sides of peat.

There are several routes that can be taken from here: the bottom of the clough is reasonably wide and it is often easier in dry periods to work up this section by using the boulders as stepping stones, instead of using the clough sides which are steep and do not provide any easier purchase for boots. Continue along as the sides of this long cleft converge inwards and become steeper. You also encounter the first in a series of vertical faces across the clough which form the waterfalls and the main obstacles to be overcome during your ascent. A rope is not needed, unless it is for confidence; simple study can help select a line up Wildboar Clough and where this is

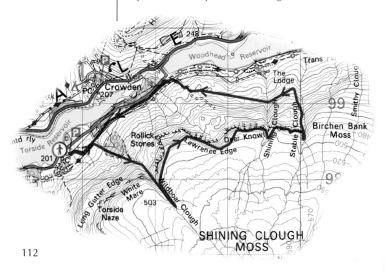

It is possible to navigate around the scrambles

difficult to detect or the flow of water does not permit progress, alternative routes are available on the north-eastern slope. At the top the route starts to level out and the stream becomes wider with miniature waterfalls. ▶

At the top a low wall, short in length, on the left hand side of the clough indicates where the path to Lawrence Edge begins. Take this route through heather and work your way along keeping the eroded peat haggs well to the right so as not to stray too far inland. The path keeps the crags to its left and threads in and out of successive cloughs and a line of gritstone edges stretching from **Lawrence Edge** in the west to Dowstone Rocks in the east, finally arriving at the turning circle at the top of the shooting track coming up **Stable Clough**.

> **Lawrence Edge** is well known for its climbing routes yet it is a good deal quieter than the honeypots of Stanage and Froggatt Edges. It also gives excellent views along the Longdendale Valley, an ancient packhorse route dating from the medieval period

These provide a perfect place to sit and rest after all that effort in the ascent.

Dowstone Rocks, a quieter gritstone edge

when salt from the Cheshire mines was transported over to Yorkshire.

Turn left from the vehicle circle and follow the track down to a gate barring the way bearing the notice 'Private no Access' even though it gives out onto open access moorland. Further signs direct the walker towards Shining Clough; take note of the one advising 'Follow fence to access road'. Following this instruction will avoid any confusion with the landowners. Follow the fence west across open moorland to a small wood at **Shining Clough**. Cross the brook and carry straight on west along the fence line. Do not go right and down through the woodland. The line of the fence eventually brings you to a track leading down the hillside towards the Longdendale Trail. On reaching the tarmac road by a row of dilapidated houses go straight across in front of the houses to then turn left and onto the Longdendale Trail and the return back to **Torside car park**.

WALK 20
Old Glossop to Bleaklow Head

Start/Finish	Shepley Street, Old Glossop, SK 045 948
Distance	13km (8 miles)
Ascent	577m
Time	4hrs
Terrain	Open moorland, footpaths and tracks
Map	OS 1:25000 Explorer OL1 Dark Peak
Parking	Shepley Street, Old Glossop, SK 045 948

Old Glossop is a good place to start and rest after the walk to Bleaklow Head, with its large cairn and photo opportunity among the numerous gritstone sculptures formed by the wind. The high point of the walk for many people will be the wreck of the Boeing B29 Superfortress that crashed on the plateau in 1948. It is spread over a wide area and is certainly something to be experienced. Please take only pictures and be respectful at the site. Higher Shelf Stones has a triangulation pillar with many high-quality graffiti chiselled into the rock.

From the turning circle at the end of Shepley Street walk up Hope Street, keeping the mill buildings on your left. After Hope Street turns left take the next right, Charles Lane, up to a wooden gate. Go through the gate to enter a sunken lane between two walls and carry on along the lane and through a second gate to arrive at the corner of a forest plantation. Take the footpath through the gate running between the Blakemoor Plantation and a wall. Go straight across an area of open ground to a second forest plantation and continue along the footpath between plantation and wall. At the end of this plantation the footpath descends back into the sunken lane through a gate on the right hand side by the wall, then carries on up the hillside and, just after crossing a tumbledown wall, turns right through a wooden gate and

*The Wain Stones
(Kissing Stones)
Bleaklow*

heads out across open moorland on a vehicle track up to the old quarries ahead.

Stay on the vehicle track heading exactly northeast, passing a line of grouse butts on the

WRECK OF THE B29

At first sight the wreck of the B29 is difficult to take in, being so large and so spread out. It is one of many within the Dark Peak, its topography causing many an aircraft to fly too low. The USAF Boeing RB-29A Superfortress crashed on its way to the base at Burtonwood, with the loss of all 13 crew on 3 November 1948. A memorial was erected in 1988 and a service is conducted at the site each year on Armistice Day. There are two more crash sites further along the route at James Thorn (see Appendix C for a full list of the sites). Please do not remove or disturb any material from or around the crash sites.

right, until you reach the remains of a building where a second track joins from the left. Go straight ahead in the direction of the waymark post to join the Pennine Way at **Clough Edge** with Torside Clough above. Turn right and follow the Pennine Way up **Torside Clough** to the Pennine Way waymark post pointing down to Wildboar Grain. Follow the waymark sign, going down to the stream and crossing both streams to walk up the footpath on the left hand side of Wildboar Grain with the path winding this way and that as it follows the stream uphill to reach the cairn at **Bleaklow Head**.

From Bleaklow Head take the footpath southwest to the Wain Stones, two gritstone boulders which when viewed from a certain perspective look as though they are kissing each other, and also the summit of Bleaklow at 633m. ▸

This is the second highest point in the Peak District after Kinder Scout.

After reaching the Wain Stones go directly south to Hern Stones and then southsouthwest for 500 metres to reach the site of the B29 Aircraft crash.

A further 200 metres in a south-westerly direction will bring you to

Higher Shelf Stones triangulation pillar

the triangulation pillar at **Higher Shelf Stones**. Take the footpath west from Higher Shelf Stones to Lower Shelf Stones maintaining height along the edge at all times and continuing along the footpath to **James's Thorn**, then descend southwest down a grass track to reach a stile in a wire fence. Go over the stile and continue downhill to a gap in a wall by grouse butts below **Shelf Benches**. Go through the gap and aim for the corner of a walled enclosure ahead, proceeding straight on along the track with the enclosures on the right and the track becoming a stone vehicle track. Pass through two farm gates and after the second gate, at the junction with two bridges over streams, take the track over the right hand bridge and cross farmland, passing through two gates to arrive back at the turning circle on Shepley Street in **Old Glossop**.

WALK 21
Kinder Scout Northern Edge

Start/Finish	Birchen Clough car park, A57, SK 109 914
Distance	22km (14 miles)
Ascent	706m
Time	7hrs
Terrain	Moorland footpaths and rocky terrain
Map	OS 1:25000 Explorer OL1 Dark Peak
Parking	Birchen Clough car park, A57, SK 109 914

This walk introduces you to the northern edge of the Kinder Plateau via Ashop Clough, a beautiful, gently rising clough at its best when the heather is in full bloom. The main part of the walk along the northern edge of Kinder gives wide-ranging views over to Bleaklow and the Upper Derwent Valley. The second half of the walk follows the old Roman road passing little-known rock features and hidden cloughs. In winter, on a clear day with blue skies, there is nowhere better in the Dark Peak from which to experience winter walking.

From the Birchen Clough car park cross the A57 Snake Road and enter Snake Woodlands. Follow the footpath through a wooden gate and into woodland with the stream on your left to reach a wooden footbridge. Cross the bridge and continue through the trees to a concrete bridge over the stream on your right. Go straight ahead into trees keeping the stream on the right and follow the footpath to a gate, which leads on to a second wooden footbridge. Cross this to a footpath leading up **Ashop Clough** and signposted 'Snake Path to Hayfield'.Follow the path and pass through two gates to enter **Black Ashop Moor**.

Continue rising gently along the path, crossing several fords and passing a small pond on your right, to the remains of a small building with a footbridge below it.

Take the right hand path
that rises above the ruins
and proceed along the clough
eventually meeting the course
of the River Ashop. Make the best of
the line by keeping to the drier areas and keeping on a
general westerly heading. Eventually a stone path emerges
heading southwest and this takes you to the Pennine Way
marker post.

At the post turn left, southeast, and ascend to the
Kinder Plateau by the excellent stone path to a large cairn
at the top. Walking past the cairn for 30 metres turn left,
east, and work through the peat groughs to a new sheep
fence and stile. Cross the stile and continue east until you
pick up **The Edge** path no more than 50 metres from the
fence. The footpath keeps to the edge of the plateau for
3km eventually arriving at **Fairbrook Naze**. ◄

*This is an amazing
viewpoint looking
over the Woodlands
Valley and across to
the high moors of
Bleaklow, Howden
and Derwent.*

The **Kinder Plateau** is subject to some of the worst
weather in the UK, especially in winter. There is
very little in the way of windbreaks across the area
and this, along with the rain, snow and ice, has
resulted in some fantastical shapes in the gritstone.
Some spectacular examples are passed going east

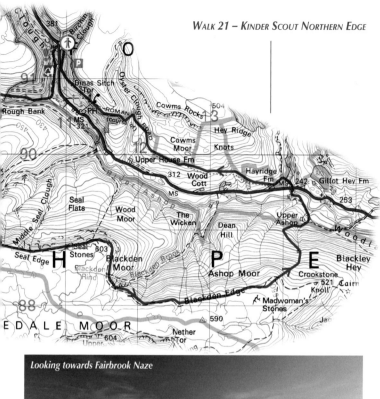

Looking towards Fairbrook Naze

The Boxing Gloves

towards Fairbrook Naze. The most famous of these is the Boxing Gloves, unmistakeable when you see them, standing as sentinels looking out to the north.

The footpath heads south for 750 metres, then crosses **Fair Brook** to turn east reaching **Seal Stones** after 2.6km. From here the direction once again turns south and passes through a gate then fords **Blackden Brook** before heading east along **Blackden Edge** for 2.4km to reach spot height 555m (marked on the 1:25000 OS map) where the path splits.

The clough has a shooting cabin at its foot, dating from 1935.

Take the path heading northeast, with views up the Alport Valley opposite. Follow the path until a second path intersects, then follow a line of grouse butts along a tumbledown wall, descending the hillside to a small clough heading north. ◄

From the shooting cabin take the track northwest to a second track and follow it right, to a farmhouse. Do not go in the farmyard but go right by the farm gate and cross a small stream to reach the farm track. Turn right along the track then first left down a sunken lane, going through a gate to finish at a ford over the **River Ashop**. Cross the river here and proceed through the gate onto the A57 Snake Road.

Go through a gate opposite into a wooded lane leading to a stone stile and footpath going up to a second wooden gate and field to a signpost on a farm track. Turn left to enter **Hayridge Farm** and then go right between two buildings, and through two farm gates to ascend a wide track up fields to a wooden gate by a wall with woodland to the left. Continue following the wall through fields to a wooden stile to **Knots**. Walk along the track keeping the wall on your left through two wooden gates to reach **Cowms Moor**. Cross the moor towards the forest plantation and after crossing a wooden stile follow the track right, to a second wooden stile and continue to a wide stream by a sheepfold. Go over the stile and descend to ford the stream in the bottom of **Oyster Clough**, following the wall on the left up the other side to reach a forest plantation.

Here the route joins what the OS map describes as the course of a **Roman road**. There is certainly evidence that a Roman route may well have existed here, connecting the Roman settlements of Navio at Brough in the Hope Valley and Melandra at Glossop, via Hope Cross and Doctor's Gate leading from Bleaklow.

The footpath follows the line of a wall on the left before entering the forest over a wooden stile. Take the footpath straight ahead to walk below **Dinas Sitch Tor**. The woodland here was cleared at the time of writing, the hillside denuded of trees. Eventually the footpath descends to the A57 but our route bears right up the forest track to arrive back at the car park at Birchen Clough.

WALK 22

Kinder Scout Western Edge

Start/Finish	Bowden Bridge car park, Hayfield, SK 048 869
Distance	13.5km (8 miles)
Ascent	575m
Time	5hrs
Terrain	Rocky terrain, open moorland, footpaths and tracks
Map	OS 1:25000 Explorer OL1 Dark Peak
Refreshments	Hayfield
Parking	Bowden Bridge car park, Hayfield, SK 048 869

The first section of this walk has huge historical significance for walkers and lovers of the countryside the length and breadth of the country. The walk starts from an unassuming car park set in the remains of a quarry. Inspection of the quarry face will reveal a small plaque commemorating the Kinder Mass Trespass that set off from this very spot.

The walk follows a natural line up William Clough and onto the Kinder Plateau where it then tracks the western plateau edge before joining an ancient packhorse route to return to Bowden Bridge.

THE KINDER SCOUT MASS TRESPASS

Around 400 ramblers from Manchester gathered in the quarry on a Sunday morning, 24 April 1932, intent on walking onto the Duke of Devonshire's shooting land on the Kinder Plateau. They had been turned off Bleaklow a few weeks previously and were discontent at the lack of access to high moorland. The walkers set off up William Clough and at some point headed straight up onto the plateau, where gamekeepers, who had been given instruction to stop any walkers gaining access, were waiting. A small fracas ensued and eventually the walkers went on their way across the plateau and met up with other walkers who had set off from Edale. On their return to Hayfield six walkers were arrested and at the subsequent trial five were imprisoned for between two and six months. The Kinder Mass Trespass as it

William Clough, where the Mass Trespass strode onto Kinder Scout

became known has now passed into folklore and is celebrated each year on the same date.

The event was part of a sea change in both political and social attitudes towards recreation and public right of access to outdoor activities, especially walking. Walking had become a social movement that demanded the right to walk in the privately owned lands held by the rich and powerful. They were denied that right and mass trespass was seen as an effective avenue for demonstration. After the war the Labour government set up a commission which resulted in acts being passed by parliament giving people the right to walk across huge areas that were previously restricted. It also brought about the creation of the national parks, the first of which was the Peak National Park, now the Peak District.

From the car park turn left and follow Kinder Road to gates across the road by a bridge on the right. Note the booth sheepwash by the bridge, where sheep from Kinder Scout would be brought for washing by hand. Go through the gate and along a tarmac track with the river on the right. Where two gates block progress, go through

Clough is a term used in the Peak District to indicate a small valley with steep sides that has been cut into a hillside by a stream running in the bottom.

the left hand gate, up a stone path bounded with walls to where the left hand wall finishes with a view of Kinder Reservoir and Kinder Scout. Turn left at a bridleway sign and follow the track up to go through a gate in a wall. At the signpost for the Snake Inn turn right and follow the footpath with a wall on the right eventually dropping down the hillside at Nab Brow, then take the left hand path that gently descends to cross a ford at the bottom of William Clough. ◄

Turn left up **William Clough**, the path switching from side to side as it ascends to the Kinder Plateau. After 900 metres the stream forks; take the right hand fork and continue your ascent, the final section up stone steps. At the top join a broad path and go straight ahead for 100 metres then take the stone-flagged path right to join the Pennine Way and a short walk up stone steps onto the Kinder Plateau. At the top turn right and continue along the Pennine Way passing through two gates before arriving at **Kinder Downfall**.

The moors above Kinder Reservoir

Kinder Downfall is best viewed either on a windy day after heavy rainfall, when, if the wind is blowing in the correct direction, water is forced back up the waterfall and onto the plateau, or in a hard winter when the waterfall has frozen and the whole of Kinder Downfall is encased in ice. Often climbers will ascend these new ice cliffs.

127

Kinder Downfall doing its party piece

Cross the waterfall at a suitable point and go south along the edge, crossing a second waterfall at **Red Brook** before coming to **Kinder Low triangulation pillar**. From this point head south, the path becoming stone flags. Here a short diversion can be made southwest along a natural spur, leading to a superb viewpoint with Kinderlow Cavern below. Retrace your steps to the Pennine Way passing an ancient burial barrow on your left. Continue along the stone walkway with Edale Rocks in the distance on your left. Eventually the path follows the line of a wall on the right to Swine's Back and then goes through a gate to the bridleway at **Edale Cross**.

Edale Cross marks the boundary of the former Royal Forest and sits on the Hayfield to Edale bridleway, an ancient route across the moor. The cross is one of many wayside crosses from the medieval period that were used to mark important routes and also as a religious waymark showing the way to religious sites and funeral routes between settlements.

From Edale Cross follow the bridleway right, down the hillside, passing through three farm gates to a farm track at **Coldwell Clough** then down a tarmac lane leading past a stone farmhouse and outbuildings on the right. Carry on until you reach the valley floor where the lane goes through a gate marked 'Walkers Only', and continues to a junction with a lane coming down from the right. Go left at this junction and follow the tarmac lane through farmland and across a cattle grid to a bridge across a river. Cross the bridge and turn left down the road, following its course around a left hand bend to a second bridge which, when crossed, brings you back to **Bowden Bridge car park**.

Edale Cross on the old Packhorse route to Hayfield

129

WALK 23

Kinder Scout

Start/Finish	Edale car park SK 123 853
Distance	16km (10 miles)
Ascent	520m
Time	5hrs
Terrain	Open moorland and steep rocky terrain
Map	OS 1:25000 Explorer OL1 Dark Peak
Refreshments	Edale
Parking	Edale car park SK 123 853

No book about walks in the Dark Peak would be complete without a walk to Kinder Scout, the Peak District's highest point. To get there, however, you have to undertake a journey that has defeated many and thrilled the successful. Kinder Scout is shrouded in legend from the Mass Trespass in the 1930s. Its peat bogs and groughs have long passed into mythology: the deep incisions in the peat can have the consistency of a chocolate fondant and confound navigation, trap the unwary and exasperate the desperate. At any time of year Kinder Scout is a place of extreme beauty, but this walk does require excellent navigation skills, for once you have left the scarily named Madwoman's Stones there are no markers and no footpaths and almost no points of reference.

From the car park walk up the road and under the railway bridge to reach the village. Just before the Old Nags Head pub, on the opposite side of the road, you will see a gate marking the official start of the Pennine Way. Continue straight on past the pub, following the road then track, until progress is blocked by an iron gate leading onto a private drive. Take the footpath to the right of the gate, signposted Grindsbrook, and descend to a wooden footbridge. Cross the footbridge over the river then go through a gate and up stone steps to follow the stone-flagged path heading towards Grindsbrook Clough for

100 metres. Take the concessionary path right across the field up to Heardman's Plantation. At the wall go through the gate and turn right up stone steps and follow the clear path as it zig zags its way up **The Nab** towards Ringing Roger. Just after the path goes directly north it forks, the left going to Golden Clough; take the right hand fork, which leads northeast up the nose of **Ringing Roger** via an easy scramble.

The old Pennine Way up Grindsbrook

> The gritstone at the top of **Ringing Roger** illustrates the sedimentary process that formed the Dark Peak gritstone over millions of years. Layer upon layer of silt flowed down into the delta that formed when the landmass sat near the equator. Successive out-pourings of material built up on top of each other resulting in today's formations.

At the top of Ringing Roger admire the view then take the short length of stone-flagged path northeast past a wire fence, the stone flags now gone, and where the path forks take the left hand footpath across moorland to the gritstone formation known as the Druid's Stone, situated on the left hand side of the footpath. ▶

The Druid's Stone is so called because it was used as a ceremonial altar for offerings placed in recesses on top of the boulder during worship by the Druids.

131

Walk on 260 metres and then take the right hand footpath at the path fork before following the moorland path north passing a collection of large gritstone boulders on the way to a fork in the footpath. Take the left hand path and at the next junction again go left. Continue until you reach a clear intersection of four paths by a large boulder on the right. Take the south-west path up across open moorland to the **Madwoman's Stones** clearly visible on the horizon.

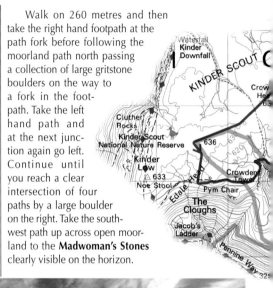

Madwoman's Stone

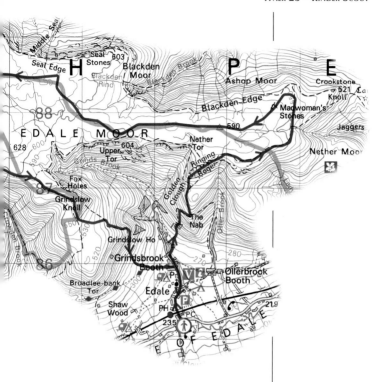

Madwoman's Stones stand proud and isolated at the eastern end of the Kinder Plateau. Their name derives from the story about a local woman who, when jilted by her lover, came to this isolated spot and – distraught with grief at her loss – bashed her head on the stones to escape the pain of having loved and lost. Many gritstone formations in the Dark Peak have names, useful for navigation as well as telling a story. Noe Stool, for instance, sits by the source of the River Noe; Pym Chair is named after a local dignitary; and Woolpacks are so named because they look like bales of wool.

MADWOMAN'S STONE TO THE SUMMIT

This next section of the route, the walk through the interior of the plateau to the summit of Kinder Scout, is the crux of the day's walk. It is a test of navigation as there are few landmarks from which to get your bearings. If you are uncertain, think carefully about entering the interior. Different routes can be taken; the one described here is one of the nicest and easiest to navigate.

The bearings and distances are taken from the OS map and used to plot the course; the features and spot heights mentioned appear on the 1:25000 OS map. Proceed as follows:

- take a bearing of 240 degrees from the western tip of Madwoman's Stones and walk for 650 metres to a point shown on the 1:25000 OS map as a civil boundary (the black dots)
- then 302 degrees for 150 metres to arrive at the triangulation pillar named Edale Moor
- then 254 degrees for 250 metres
- then 295 degrees for 300 metres
- then 257 degrees for 400 metres to arrive at the smaller of two knolls at grid reference SK 1203 8780
- from this grid reference head 277 degrees for 300 metres following the civil boundary on the OS map
- then 237 degrees for 220 metres to arrive at the 604m spot height at Hartshorn
- then 288 degrees for 575 metres to a small knoll, grid reference SK 1100 8791, the gateway to the Eye of the Needle.

From the knoll the objective is to navigate between the two small streams that converge to leave a narrow gap in which to thread yourself through without getting wet feet. Take a bearing of 318 degrees and walk across the moor for 550 metres, passing a collection of gritstone boulders on your right and passing between two small streams. Depending on the weather, water may or may not be present. From here:

- go directly north for 150 metres to reach gritstone boulders at the head of **Blackden Rind**
- then walk directly west for 850 metres to feed the route through the second needle at grid reference SK 0981 8846
- from this point head 215 degrees for 400 metres passing through a boulderfield to arrive at **Crowden Head** denoted by a stake at grid reference SK 0957 8814, spot height 632m
- take a bearing of 226 degrees and proceed for 550 metres
- then 259 degrees for 700 metres to reach the spot height of 636m at grid reference SK 0851 8752.

This is generally accepted as the summit of the Kinder Scout plateau. ▶

Walk on a bearing of 143 degrees for 200 metres to a rockfield and then directly south at 180 degrees for 330 metres to reach the edge path between Noe Stool and **Pym Chair** rock formations. Turn left and walk along the edge path heading east for 2.1km stopping just before Grindsbrook Clough at the junction of the stone path leading to Grindslow Knoll. Go right, down the stone flags and just before the path starts its ascent to **Grindslow Knoll** take the faint footpath right leading down to skirt along a wire sheep fence culminating in a gate. Go through the gate and after five metres take the footpath heading east towards the corner of a wall. Continue to follow the wall along, almost due east, until you reach a wide track heading down from Grindslow Knoll. Go right here and follow the track down to a wooden gate at an access point. Go through the gate and left diagonally down the field to the lane. Join the lane onto the Pennine Way and return to **Edale** passing through two gates, the final one being the decorated gateway for the start of the Pennine Way.

After the summit it is a short distance to the edge path and the route back to Edale.

WALK 24
Kinder Scout Southern Edge

Start/Finish	Edale car park SK 123 853
Distance	13km (8 miles)
Ascent	546m
Time	5hrs
Terrain	Moorland footpaths and steep rocky terrain
Map	OS 1:25000 Explorer OL1 Dark Peak
Refreshments	Edale
Parking	Edale car park SK 123 853

This walk follows the original start of the Pennine Way across Grinds Brook, using the famous log footbridge to enter Grindsbrook Clough, which delivers you onto the Kinder Plateau. Once on the top, be wary of sheep exacting a toll from exhausted walkers. The route gives superb views across to the Great Ridge, along with one of the interesting features of this part of the Kinder Plateau, the many and varied forms of natural stone sculpture carved by wind, rain and ice. The walk takes you through tiny hamlets to return to Edale.

From the car park walk up the road and under the railway bridge to reach the village. Just before the Old Nags Head pub, on the opposite side of the road, you will see a gate marking the start of the Pennine Way. Continue straight on past the pub, following the road then track, until progress is blocked by an iron gate leading onto a private drive. Take the footpath to the right of the gate, signposted Grindsbrook, and descend to the wooden footbridge across Grinds Brook. Cross and ascend the other

side through a gate, then along a stone-flagged footpath to a wood in the distance. At the wood go through the gate and follow the footpath winding its way through the trees to exit via a second gate.

Look from the top of Grindsbrook

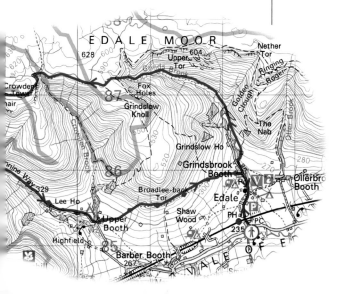

Turn immediately left and cross the footbridge over the stream coming down from **Golden Clough**, then bear left to follow the clear footpath up Grindsbrook Clough keeping the brook on your left. After passing through a gate in a sheep fence the footpath meanders to the left and right of **Grinds Brook** leaving the walker to find the best and most suitable route. As you approach the top, the clough narrows significantly and the terrain becomes rocky, requiring judgement and good route choice as you pick your way up to the top. Do not veer off the main clough: ignore all tributaries and you will eventually pop out at the top. ◄

Take a rest, you have earned it, but keep an eye out for the sheep stealing your sandwiches.

Kinder Scout at 636m is the highest point in the Peak District. The plateau is ringed by gritstone edges formed between 360 million and 300 million years ago when sediments were continuously deposited above the limestone bed laid down when this part of the world was on the equator. The interior of the plateau is predominantly peat moorland and bog made from rotting vegetation and sphagnum mosses. Where water has eroded the peat, deep incisions called groughs have formed producing this unique landscape.

From the top of Grindsbrook Clough take the stone-flagged path west along the southern edge of the plateau. The stone flags eventually stop, the footpath continuing to Crowden Clough on peat. At Crowden Clough cross **Crowden Brook** by the ford and then ascend stone steps to arrive at **Crowden Tower**. ◄ The path now works its way through, over and around fantastical rock formations with names such as the Woolpacks, Pym Chair and Noe Stool at the head of the River Noe. From **Noe Stool** proceed 200 metres southwest and, where the footpath fords a stream coming from the right, turn right and follow the stream upwards over the moor. Where the stream forks take the left hand tributary and follow its course for 160 metres to arrive at the triangulation pillar for **Kinder Low**.

There are magnificent views along the Vale of Edale and across to Mam Tor.

From the triangulation pillar follow cairns along the Pennine Way generally south east to Edale Rocks. From here the route goes to the left of Swine's Back, the footpath becoming stone-flagged and descending south across moorland. Where the path levels out take the left hand fork down to a cairn above **Jacob's Ladder** with a signpost indicating 'Public Footpath by Jacob's Ladder left to Edale'. Take this route and descend the stone footpath to a stone bridge over a stream at the bottom. Go over the bridge and then immediately right, through a gate and onto a track. Proceed along the track passing through successive gates to reach **Lee House** on the left with a National Trust shelter and information point on the right. Pass the cottages on the left and follow the tarmac road down to **Upper Booth**.

There are several 'booths' in the Vale of Edale. A **booth** was originally a cattle-rearing place, usually just a shed or small building that provided shelter. The booths date from the 13th century and were known then as 'vaccaries', places where sheep or cattle are kept.

At Upper Booth farm and campsite go left through the farmyard, then right between barn and wall and then left to a Pennine Way signpost pointing to Edale in the east. Follow the Pennine Way across fields, rising slightly in front of **Broadlee-bank Tor** then dropping across fields and through numerous gates to the sunken lane heading right down to the Old Nags Head pub at **Grindsbrook Booth**. Continue to the road and turn right to return to the car park in **Edale**.

WALK 25

The Great Ridge

Start/Finish	Castleton, National Park Visitor Centre, SK 149 829
Distance	12km (7½ miles)
Ascent	480m
Time	4hrs
Terrain	Open moorland, footpaths and tracks
Map	OS 1:25000 Explorer OL1 Dark Peak
Refreshments	Castleton
Parking	Public pay and display car park SK 149 829

The Great Ridge walk is one of the classic day's out in the Dark Peak. The Great Ridge running from Lose Hill in the northeast to Mam Tor in the southwest sits on the very edge of the Dark Peak, with Mam Tor, a mountain made of shale, bridging the geological gap between Dark and White Peak. The route can be busy on sunny days as the views from the ridge are magnificent. Descending from Mam Tor via the limestone of Cave Dale, the walk passes below Peveril Castle, a former Norman stronghold.

Leave the National Park Visitor Centre and turn left into the village. Follow the main road around a sharp left hand bend then at the next bend do not turn right but carry straight on to Millbridge. Proceed down the lane until you come to the right hand fork in the road to Hollowford Outdoor Centre and follow the walled track past the centre on the left to a gate by a cattle grid across the track. Go through the gate and immediately take the footpath signposted on the right crossing two fields with picket gates to reach a lane.

Go straight on following the signpost for Lose Hill, passing through three farm gates to join a road with a signpost to Lose Hill and Hope. Turn left and walk up the road to the right of the stone house and go through the picket gate to ascend a concrete farm track. Where the track meets a picket gate on your left, go through the gate and up the fields following the signpost for Lose Hill until you reach a gate in a wall to join a footpath coming uphill from the right. Turn left up the footpath until you come to a stile on your right in a wire fence. Cross the stile and bear left uphill to cross a stile to continue on to the summit of **Lose Hill**.

Lose Hill is also known on the Ordnance Survey map as Ward's Piece. GHB Ward was the secretary of the Sheffield Clarion Ramblers who, along with their fellow ramblers in

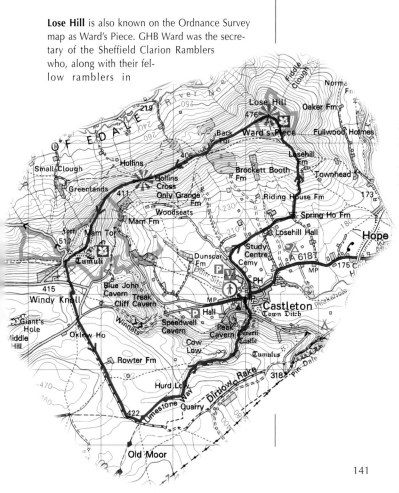

The Great Ridge to Mam Tor

Manchester, campaigned for access to the moors and hills around Derbyshire. The activities of the local rambling clubs were instrumental in the formation of the Peak National Park. Lose Hill was purchased by the Sheffield Clarion Ramblers and given to GHB Ward, who bequeathed it to the National Trust.

Turn left and head southwest along the Great Ridge. The path is well-defined and easy going in most sections: the section at Back Tor requires care as it has a steep descent but it is not difficult. There are several stiles and gates along the ridge path; as long as you stay on the ridge you will not lose your way. After **Back Tor** the path descends to **Hollins Cross**.

Hollins Cross is a natural point between the two valleys of Edale and Hope. The only burial site used to be in Hope in the Hope Valley. Coffins were carried over Hollins Cross from Edale, the route becoming known as a Coffin Route. The practice ceased when the church was built at Edale.

From Hollins Cross the path now starts its ascent to **Mam Tor**, the highest point of the walk at 517m.

> **Mam Tor** is made up of shale and sandstone, parts of which were laid down some 320 million years ago. The layers of shale lower down the hill make the land beneath the summit unstable, and evidence of the numerous landslips that have occurred can be seen at its base. The summit also marks the location of ancient forts and burial sites dating back to the Bronze Age.

From the summit take the footpath southwest down to a gate leading onto a road. Go through the gate and turn immediately left down to a second gate leading out onto a field. Cross this field and the road beyond to another field with a track. Continue along the track until you reach a road. ▶ Cross the road and bear right then left to a farm gate leading to a tarmac track. Go through the gate and up the track, keeping the wall on your left. Continue along the track, ignoring the ladder stile on

Note that the geological landscape has now changed from gritstone and shale to limestone.

Cave Dale and the start of White Peak

your left, to a junction with a second track running from your right.

Turn left along the track and go through the farm gate. Turn left, signposted '**Limestone Way**', and follow the marked trail through a farm gate and across fields to a signpost marked 'Public Bridleway to Cave Dale'. Go through the gate in the wall and along the footpath to a second gate that leads into Cave Dale. Descend into Cave Dale and where the footpath forks keep right to enter the narrow gorge with limestone cliffs and outcrops on either side. Take care in wet weather as the limestone can be slippery. Towards the bottom of Cave Dale, **Peveril Castle** can be seen high up on the left. At the bottom of Cave Dale, go through the gate and then left to reach the village green. Go left of the green and then right past the **church** to arrive on the main road. Turn left to return to the National Park Visitor Centre and the end of the walk.

> **Castleton** has a number of attractions, along with a cluster of tea rooms, cafés and trinket shops. Peveril Castle is open every day and is reached from the road just opposite the National Park Visitor Centre. There are also several caves that can be visited by the public, including the famous Blue John Cavern, situated near Mam Tor, known for its semi-precious Blue John fluorite.

NORTHERN DARK PEAK

Laddow Rocks and the Crowden Valley (Walk 28)

The north of the Dark Peak can often seem bleak at first glance. It has desolate moorlands intersected by deeply incised valleys, fringed with towering gritstone edges that sit above boulder-strewn hillsides. Enter this landscape and you will find yourself walking across beautiful moorland with wildlife and plantlife in abundance and stunning views across deep valleys. It is less frequented than the more famous parts of the Dark Peak so the walker can have a day's walking within a few miles of major cities and not see a soul.

These northern moors and gritstone edges have seen a major programme of improvement in recent years thanks to the work of Moors For The Future. Consequentially the land has become wetter, bringing with it greater diversity of plantlife and an end to the erosion of the peat, as grasses take root and hold this precious material in place.

A walk across these moors is a thing of beauty these days. Take Black Hill: noted for being a quagmire in the 1970s, it is now a place of cottongrass and sedges and green rather than black. It is also a place of hidden delights in the wonderful cloughs that abound to the north. Ramsden and Birchin Cloughs are two of the most awe-inspiring cloughs in the whole of the Peak District and must be visited.

WALK 26
Dunford Bridge to Ramsden Clough

Start/Finish	Dunford Bridge SE 158 023
Distance	18.5km (11½ miles)
Ascent	523m
Time	6hrs
Terrain	Moorland and footpaths
Map	OS 1:25000 Explorer OL1 Dark Peak
Parking	Dunford Bridge SE 158 023

This is an area of the Dark Peak often neglected by walkers, as it is not close to any major centres. The walk makes up for the lack of local amenities with two major attractions. The first is solitude. Being off the beaten track means wide open views across miles of moorland, with no one else to be seen, making for a true wilderness experience. The second is Ramsden Clough. This verdant, narrow valley is quite a shock when you arrive. After walking across moorland, with views into the Yorkshire Dales and across to the South Pennines, you suddenly arrive at a deep cleft in the landscape that is an unexpected delight.

From the car park at Dunford Bridge turn left up the road and take the first road right past the sailing club to **Winscar Reservoir**. Walk right, across the dam, and then bear left at the end to follow the road through the reservoir car park to a minor road leading uphill. Go left up the road and just before the first house on the left take the private road (walkers are permitted) on the left down to a gate. Go through the gate and continue down to cross the dam, turning right at the end by the reservoir boundary wall, and follow the vehicle track along until it forks. Take the left hand fork through old quarries and across **Lower Snailsden Moss** to a wall. Turn right before the wall and follow the track up onto Snailsden Edge until you reach a corner of a drystone wall.

Ramsden Clough: a pleasant surprise

From here make a short ascent onto the moor and head for the **triangulation pillar**, which is in plain view. From the pillar go generally northwest directly in line with the transmitter tower at Holme Moss for 440 metres to reach a vehicle track heading northeast. Follow the track across the moor and down the hillside, and after crossing a wooden bridge over Reaps Dike, go left and follow a line of grouse butts leading to the top of Ruddle Clough.

Go over the stile to the left of grouse butt number 3 to cross the fence and follow the footpath, generally southwest along the top of **Ramsden Clough**. After crossing two fords, where the path forks, take the higher path to follow a line of upright wooden panels used as grouse butts until you reach grouse butt number 8 and a vehicle track heading left towards the southeast. Follow the track to the fence on the horizon then follow the fence left until you reach a stile at the intersection of two fences. Cross the stile and with the fence on your right follow this up the hillside to reach the triangulation pillar at Dead Edge End.

Continue east along the fence until it turns southwest. From this point head southeast aiming for a concrete surveyor's pillar 580 metres away. Proceed past the pillar to the vehicle track following the line on the map of the **Woodhead Tunnel** below.

The line of the three **Woodhead tunnels** was checked using the surveyor's pillar. The first tunnel opened in 1845; the last in 1953. The last train through the tunnels was in 1981. The western end is in the Longdendale Valley, while the eastern end is at Dunford Bridge. The tunnels now carry powerlines for the National Grid.

Go right, along the track and follow it down the hillside past a redundant brick building and just after, where it joins a track at the foot of the hillside, go left to go through a gate leading onto a road. Walk right, to the junction with the A628, and then cross and go through the gate directly opposite leading onto a track. Follow the track down and at the junction with a track going generally east to west turn right and proceed westwards to **Salter's Brook** to view the ancient packhorse bridge.

Ladyshaw Bridge on the Longdendale Trail was originally used to transport salt from Cheshire. The route split at the junction beyond the bridge, one way going to Wakefield, the other towards Rotherham. In 1828 the bridge was narrowed to force traffic to use the new turnpike road, the A628. The building remains are a former public house. The milepost opposite states the distance to Wortley as XII miles and Rotherham XXI miles.

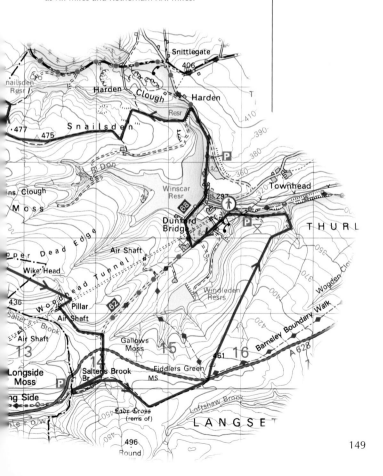

Retrace your steps up to the previous track junction and continue east over a stile to ascend the hillside to **Lady Cross**.

> **Lady Cross**, at the highest point of the packhorse trail, was a boundary post for manorial land created by the Lords of Chester. It was also used as a marker post for travellers crossing the moors. A second is situated on Bradfield Moor, some 10km away.

Keep on the track going east and go over a stile to reach the **A628** again. Go straight across the road and through the gate opposite onto **Fiddlers Green** then uphill northeast to the **triangulation pillar** at South Nab.

From the pillar go northeast to follow Long Grain Head down its lefthand side to meet grouse butts running practically north down Thurlstone Moor. Where a man-made drainage ditch turns sharp right follow its course until you reach a stone track opposite a wooden bridge going across the ditch. Turn left down the track and follow it to a picket gate to the left of a metal farm gate across the track. Go through the picket gate and continue along the track, a tall wall at your left, to the road. Turn right to return to the car park at **Dunford Bridge**.

WALK 27
Crowden Horseshoe

Start/Finish	Crowden car park SK 072 992
Distance	16km (10 miles)
Ascent	581m
Time	5hrs
Terrain	Steep ascents and descents on uneven ground, open moor, and narrow footpath with vertical exposure
Map	OS 1:25000 Explorer OL1 Dark Peak
Parking	Crowden car park SK 072 992

This is another classic walk in the Dark Peak. The Crowden Horseshoe follows a natural line out of a valley up onto a long crag edge. The feeling of space and solitude gives this walk a special character. Laddow Rocks, on the way to Black Hill, is a significant climbing venue with spectacular vertical exposure. The return half is across typical Dark Peak moorland: wild, desolate and often windswept. The walk does not fail in giving a proper Dark Peak day out, reminiscent of the early days of rambling in the area.

From Crowden car park on the A628 take the footpath to the caravan site entrance and where the path meets a wide track go left and proceed through two wooden gates. Walk up a tarmac track until you come to a signpost pointing right to the **Pennine Way**. Follow the sign in a general northwesterly direction across three stiles and one gate to arrive at a plantation with a memorial cairn by the footpath.

Continue along the edge of the woodland to open moorland. From where the woodland stops the path enters the valley bowl and continues for 1km gently rising to a ford a stream. After crossing the stream the path ascends rocky ground fording several streams and climbing ever higher above the valley floor. Eventually, after crossing the brook at **Oaken Clough** and walking along

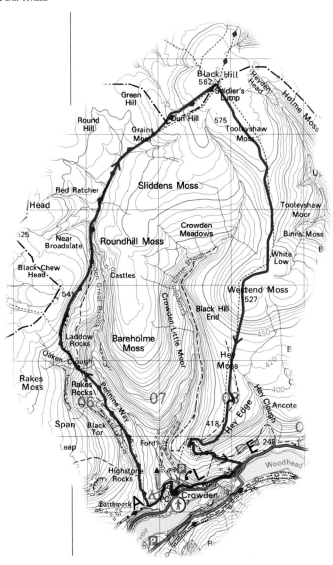

Laddow Rocks

a section of stone slabs the path reaches the top where it splits in two. Take the right hand path along the crag edge and continue. ▶ **Laddow Rocks** stretch for 1.2km with the footpath following its course before dropping back to Crowden Great Brook.

> Be careful here: pay attention at all times to the edge of the crag on the right.

> **Laddow Rocks** was an early climbing destination, popular with Manchester climbers. The rocks have many historically significant routes. A climbing accident in the 1920s resulted in the casualty being carried to the road on two No Trespassing signs, taken down by helpers. As a result of the accident a Joint Stretcher Committee was founded, one of the forerunners of the Peak District Mountain Rescue teams.

Cross **Crowden Great Brook** and turn immediately left to walk upstream, crossing where appropriate. Eventually as the footpath leaves the stream where the valley opens out onto wide flat moorland by Meadowgrain Clough, you begin the gentle ascent to Black Hill. At **Dun Hill** cross the stile and continue uphill until **Soldier's Lump** triangulation pillar comes into view signalling your arrival on **Black Hill**.

The **triangulation pillar** on Black Hill is a little confusing. Its official name is Holme Moss, which is 1km away to the southeast. Ordnance Survey maps have it down as Soldier's Lump, this name coming from the Royal Engineers who used it for surveying in the 18th century.

From Black Hill take the faint footpath a few metres back along the stone path from the triangulation pillar, and head southsoutheast over the featureless moor, eventually turning south for **Tooleyshaw Moor** and on up to White Low, passing through a line of grouse butts and a wooden stile on the way. At **White Low** the path heads west, with stakes indicating where a path lay, towards a small pool situated on **Westend Moss**.

The route heads generally south with a steep and muddy descent to **Hey Moss**. Keep well to the right of **Hey Clough** to avoid a boggy morass and look out for the abandoned triangulation pillar on Hey Edge in the distance.

Although the word '**Pillar**' is written on the map there is no accompanying blue triangle to denote a triangulation pillar. This is because it was not used in any of the surveys that followed its construction. However, it was used during a levelling survey in 1949, being 1388.99 feet above the Newlyn Datum.

From here the route goes south across open moor, then descends towards a quarry. Go right, around the quarry to its northern edge then along the narrow edge-path that leads down to the vehicle track that runs along the quarry floor. Follow this track to a cobbled track leading to a wooden stile and gate. Go over the stile and straight ahead on the cobbled track for 40 metres. Well before where the track turns left, take the footpath on the left hand side of the track and follow it southeast down through successive fields to meet a track running parallel with the A628. Turn right along the track and continue for 180 metres to arrive at St James Church.

St James Church, Woodhead

St James Church served the small community of Woodhead. Outside the churchyard are the unmarked graves of navvies killed by cholera during the construction of the Woodhead tunnels. The deceased were treated with the same disregard as they had been in life and not given a proper burial in consecrated ground. The conditions in which the navvies lived and worked were so atrocious – living in huts on Pikenaze Moor that they made from peat sods – that it contributed to the passing of new laws and the beginning of health and safety legislation in the workplace.

From the church carry on down the tarmac lane and just before the lane meets Woodhead Road go through the wooden gate on your right to cross the field. At the next wall go through the gate and follow the footpath down to a wooden gate giving access into the forest plantation. Pass through the gate and turn right following the forest path to emerge via a wooden gate in a wall, onto the lane to **Crowden car park** and the end of the walk.

WALK 28

Crowden to Chew Valley

Start/Finish	Crowden car park SK 072 992
Distance	16km (10 miles)
Ascent	630m
Time	5hrs
Terrain	Steep ascents and descents on uneven ground, open moor, narrow footpath with vertical exposure
Map	OS 1:25000 Explorer OL1 Dark Peak
Parking	Crowden car park SK 072 992

The moors between Crowden and the Chew Valley hold some superb walking with fine views. The walking is not arduous either with much along clear paths, making this option an easy, enjoyable day's walking. The route follows gritstone edges and moorland to the Chew Valley. At this height one may not be expecting to be able to stroll beside a large body of water but that is what is on offer at the Chew Reservoir and it makes for a pleasant return via Laddow Rocks to Crowden.

From Crowden car park take the footpath through trees to the entrance to the caravan site. At the junction of the footpath and the road go straight ahead through a gate opposite and follow the lane towards Crowden Outdoor Activities Centre. At the bridge go straight across and walk to the far end of the car park with the centre on your left. Take the footpath going to the right of the trees rising up steps to cross a wooden stile in a wall then walk right then left up wooden steps to a small knoll. Go straight on along a footpath, crossing a wooden footbridge, and walking up the slope to meet the Pennine Way running north.

Turn left past a small wood to a gate in a wall. Do not go through the gate but turn right to walk uphill, along a permissive footpath through three tumbledown walls. At the fourth wall turn right and follow the path uphill with the wall on your left to a stile in a wire fence. Cross the stile and continue to follow the wall for another 600 metres to the second bend in the wall and instead of following the wall southwest continue on the line of the permissive footpath, first west then northwest, the way marked by a series of cairns across open moorland to **Lad's Leap**.

The **Longdendale Valley** used to be in Cheshire and was used by the Lords of Cheshire for transporting salt from their mines over to the east of the country

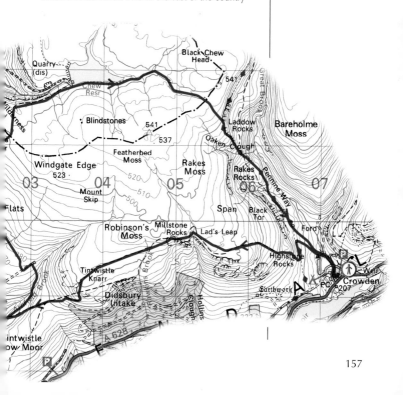

and to the port at Bawtry. When constructed in the latter half of the 19th century, the chain of reservoirs in the valley was the greatest artificial expanse of water in the world.

The remnants of the plane lie in the heather at grid reference SK 03932 99080 and are marked by a small wooden cross. Please only look and leave all items.

Cross the stream feeding into Coombes Clough and proceed along the top of **Millstone Rocks** to cross Black Gutter. Carry straight on to Robinson's Spring Reservoirs and from there in the same direction to reach a sunken track running downhill to your left. As you work your way across **Tintwistle Knarr** seek out the wreckage of a Lightning aircraft that crashed in 1944, sadly with the loss of life. ◄

Turn left down the track and follow its winding course to a wooden stile. Cross the stile and keep walking down the track until you reach a small abandoned reservoir. From the reservoir follow the footpath downhill towards **Arnfield Brook** for 650 metres and look closely on your right to spot an overgrown sunken trail heading

Lightning Air Crash Site Tintwistle Knarr

Waterfall, Arnfield Clough

northeast up Arnfield Clough, which you should take. Cross the brook at a ford 100 metres downstream of a waterfall and ascend the hillside to continue along the footpath working its way along the clough, eventually swinging away from the brook and climbing up the hillside to reach the shooting cabins viewed earlier.

Turn left along the vehicle track and where the track crosses a stream on a small concrete bridge turn right to walk across open moorland and several groughs to join a wire fence running northeast on your right. Keep company with the fence across **Arnfield Flats** until you come to a stile marked with a small cairn; this is before the permissive path marked on the OS map. Take the footpath across the stile up **Ormes Moor** and along the trail clearly marked with a line of wooden posts until you reach a level area known as **Wilderness**. Go directly north to the path overlooking Chew Valley, the junction marked with a large cairn and waymarker post. Turn right and follow the edge path up to the **Chew Reservoir**. ▸

The Chew Valley was famous as a climbing venue in the 1950s for the Manchester climbing fraternity, with many of the climbers going on to explore the Himalaya in later years.

Coming out of the Wilderness at Chew Valley

Go to the right of the dam and, keeping the reservoir on your left, follow the footpath along its shoreline to a small wooden bridge opposite a low concrete structure. Ford the stream to reach the structure and follow the course of the water upstream along a footpath, at times indistinct, but always along the line of the stream until at Laddow Moss you arrive at a stile in a wire fence. Cross the stile and follow the footpath down to **Laddow Rocks** overlooking Crowden Great Brook in the valley below.

Just before reaching the path on Laddow Rocks pay attention to the ground you are walking on and look for a **flat rock** at the side of the path that has a very small dull rounded rivet head upon it. This is a rivet placed by Ordnance Survey surveyors during the mapping of the area and marks a survey point.

Turn right and follow the Pennine Way down into the valley, keeping to the National Trail until you reach the footpath leading up from Crowden Outdoor Activities Centre that you ascended at the beginning of the walk. Turn left down the path and retrace your earlier steps back to Crowden car park.

WALK 29

Marsden to Black Hill

Start/Finish	Marsden SE 049 115
Distance	22km (13½ miles)
Ascent	675m
Time	7hrs
Terrain	Open moorland, footpaths and tracks
Map	OS 1:25000 Explorer OL1 Dark Peak
Refreshments	Marsden
Parking	Marsden station SE 048 118

The walk from Marsden to Black Hill follows the Pennine Way as it threads its way through valleys and across moorland. Marsden, like many other Pennine towns, has seen changing fortunes since the heady days of woollen textile production. Now it is resurgent with shops, restaurants and bars. The beginning of the walk takes you past beautiful mill cottages and out onto the moors, where reservoirs were built to supply water to the growing populations. As the walk progresses the moors become more remote, giving that sense of solitude unique to Dark Peak moorland.

Setting off from the Marsden information centre walk southeast down Peel Street to the junction with the **A62** and turn right down the road, then left at the next junction down Fall Lane, signposted 'Butterley Reservoir and Spillway'. At the small roundabout by Marsden Football Club ground go straight on and up Binn Road and take the cobbled lane between two towering mill buildings.

> **Bank Bottom Mill** was the largest of 13 mills in Marsden. At 14 acres it was the largest mill owned by a single individual in the world. It produced woollen textiles from 680 looms and employed almost 2000 people in its heyday. It closed in 2003.

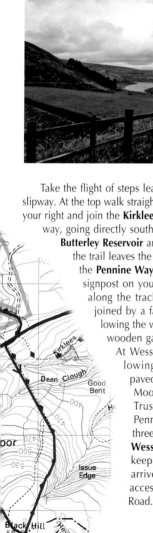

Looking back towards Marsden from the Wessenden Reservoirs

Take the flight of steps leading up by the reservoir slipway. At the top walk straight on with a stone wall on your right and join the **Kirklees Way** and public bridleway, going directly south along the edges of both **Butterley Reservoir** and **Blakeley Reservoir**. As the trail leaves the second reservoir it meets the **Pennine Way** marked by a prominent signpost on your right. Keep straight on along the track and where the trail is joined by a farm track keep right following the waymarked trail through a wooden gate at Wessenden Lodge. At Wessenden Dam go left following the trail up a stone paved track onto the Marsden Moor Estate of the National Trust. Continue along the Pennine Way Trail, crossing three wooden bridges, and at **Wessenden Head Reservoir** keep left along the track to arrive at a steel gate giving access onto Wessenden Head Road.

The **steel picture frame** is part of a joint collaboration between local artist Ashley Jackson and the National Trust. The artist's line 'Many people look, but only few see' is an attempt to encourage the onlooker to view the changing landscape through the frame and to really take in what they see.

Go through the gate and turn right, down to the road to its junction with the A635. Cross the road and turn right and walk for 150 metres then take the Pennine Way footpath left towards Black Hill. Cross the moor keeping to the Pennine Way, which alternates between peat footpath and stone slabs to reduce erosion. The path gently traverses the hillside fording several streams, the largest of which is the one in **Dean Clough**. ◀ After 1.4km the path turns directly south and heads steeply up the hill to the right of Issue Clough and deposits you on **Black Hill**.

In times of heavy rain a diversion from the road via the Kirklees Way leads to a footbridge lower down the clough, giving safe passage across.

Today **Black Hill** is surrounded by heather and cottongrass, making it a wonderful place to rest for a while, but this has not always been the case. The triangulation pillar gives some indication of the level of erosion that took place on the hill: its base now sits a metre or so above ground level. Black Hill became famous among Pennine Way walkers, often carrying the sobriquet 'the hell of Black Hill' as the peat became a quagmire, especially in wet weather: with no way around, the Pennine Way walker was forced to try and go through the peat bog, often sinking well up to the thighs.

SOLDIER'S LUMP ACROSS TO DEAN HEAD MOSS

Take care when setting off on the next section of the walk from Soldier's Lump and make sure you walk in the correct direction by taking a compass bearing. The route across to Dean Head Moss is at times indistinct. There is a series of posts and cairns that vaguely guide the walker along.

Initially from **Soldier's Lump** the route northwest is level but shortly it drops down to a rudimentary stone shelter and then strikes out down the slope to a wide col at Dean Head. Here, choose a suitable course across the wide groughs and streams, heading for the cairn at the other side. It is possible to get across to the other side without getting your feet wet, but not usual! From the cairn the path takes you via a series of cairns and posts and a stone boundary marker to a wire fence with accompanying stone cairn, which you should follow to a stile. Go over the stile and proceed through a disused quarry then go left along the **A635** keeping well into the grass verge on this busy road, and after 320 metres cross the road to a car park.

At the car park go over the stile and walk across Featherbed Moss on a path made of stone slabs. Pass through a wooden gate and keep on the footpath that loses the slabs shortly after the gate down to **Black Moss Reservoir**. Go across Black Moss Dam and through a wooden gate onto more stone slabs that take you north-east across **Bobus** and eventually, after going through a second gate, descends a slope onto the Standedge Trail above **Redbrook Reservoir**. Go right at a stone marker post with the initials MII and follow the distinct path which ends by dropping down a small clough then rising to join Mount Road.

The **junction** of roads at this point sits on the site of a Roman signal fort on the road from Chester to York. In later years this road became a salt route, used for transporting salt from the mines in Cheshire and later still it became a popular route across the Pennines for packhorse trains.

Turn right, then immediately left down Old Mount Road, keeping to the right hand tarmac road to pass through a gate by a cattle grid and proceed down the road. The views over Marsden manifest its development, with the huge mill complex you walked through at the beginning of the walk laid out before you. After 1km take

Note the date on the stone gatepost leading into the field, 1671, and note the style of the farmhouse.

the wide track on your left, going uphill by a stone house, signposted as a footpath. At the top, walk across a stone patio in front of a house and join the footpath to the right of a stone garage building to enter a walled lane that descends through a wooden gate to a farm. ◄

Proceed straight on to the left of the house, the path leading you through a small iron gate into a field. Walk across the field staying close to the right hand stone wall and go through two gates at the bottom of the field to gain access to the hillside facing you. Go right, around the hillside, maintaining height until you come to a line of telegraph poles carrying power lines up the hillside. Turn left here and follow the poles uphill to a stile. Cross the stile and turn immediately right across the front of a farmhouse to reach a low wall with a small wooden gate giving access through the wall on your left. Go through the gate and right along the field keeping the wall initially on your right and then eventually, where the wall has fallen down, on your left to reach a wire fence in front of trees and a steep-sided clough.

Turn right at the fence and walk down to a metal gate giving access to a wooden stile on the left. Go over the stile and drop down to cross a small bridge with plastic boards across a stream. At the other side step over a stile, then walk directly to a wall and where the wall has been lowered by a waymark post, stride over the gap and turn left along the wall for a few metres.

Turn right uphill by the waymark post and follow a series of posts indicating the way, keeping a tumble-down stone wall on your left. At a fine stone barn turn left up hill and go over the stile then turn immediately right to work your way across marshy ground via a series of wooden boardwalks then finally a kissing gate which deposits you onto a farm track. Go left and follow the track down to the road. At the road cross over to the other side and take the next road sharp left by a bus stop, down to farm buildings. At the T junction turn right and proceed down the road where a gap in the wall on your right gives access to the car park at Standedge Tunnel.

The **Standedge tunnels** start from here and end in Diggle, a total distance of some 5km. There are four tunnels; three are rail. The first tunnel provided a passage for the Huddersfield Narrow Canal in 1811. Progress along the canal tunnel was by narrow boat, with men using the technique of legging (lying on planks across the bow of the boat and propelling the boat with the feet against the tunnel wall) as the tunnel was too narrow to allow for a towpath. The rail tunnel constructed in 1848 is perfectly flat to allow for water-troughs along its length, which were used to refill the steam locomotives.

The Standedge Tunnel

From the tunnel visitor centre take the footpath to Marsden; a signpost indicates that it is 0.5 miles away. Follow the path along the side of the canal basin opposite the wonderful canal warehouse. Go under the rail bridge and at the other side turn right up some stone steps onto a woodland trail. Go left along the trail following the course of the canal, and after going through a wooden gate go left to join the canal towpath heading right towards Marsden. Where the path meets the canal locks follow the road right, and return to the centre of **Marsden**.

WALK 30

Alphin Pike to Birchen Clough

Start/Finish	Dove Stone Reservoir SE 013 034
Distance	16.5km (10 miles)
Ascent	615m
Time	5hrs
Terrain	Open moorland, footpaths and tracks, edge paths and some scrambling down Birchin Clough
Map	OS 1:25000 Explorer OL1 Dark Peak
Parking	Dove Stone Reservoir SE 013 034

Hidden from view, the Chew Valley only shows a hint of its delights to the passing motorist travelling over Saddleworth Moor. It comprises towering gritstone edges, steep-sided valleys, wide moors and some of the best waterfalls in the area. It is one of the best edge walks in the Dark Peak and Birchen Clough is the jewel in the crown. Birchen Clough does require a little scramble occasionally, with one steep step to negotiate. Those who prefer going up a steep rocky section rather than coming down may wish to reverse the walk.

From Dove Stone Reservoir car park head west along Bradbury Lane passing a row of identical looking cottages. After 1.2km turn right onto Intake Lane and continue down the lane, then after passing some stone houses take the footpath left at the signpost and follow its direction up through heather to a path rising from the right with a wall facing you. Turn left and follow the footpath up, crossing a stile then proceeding along a sunken path that winds its way through heather to the triangulation pillar and shelter on **Alphin Pike**.

From the pillar go directly east for 40 metres to pick up the footpath heading southeast across Slack Head Brow. Keep on this path as it progresses across the edge, crossing a stile in a wire fence, and do not stray up onto the moor, as the views and direction will be lost. At Chew Hurdles the path eventually meets the **Wilderness** indicated by a signpost on your right. Do not go into the Wilderness but keep on your current course following the gritstone edge above the Chew Valley. Do not take the path to the valley floor but maintain your present height through peat groughs to the **Chew Reservoir dam**.

The **Chew Reservoir** was the highest in England when it was built in the early 20th century. It is a compensation reservoir used for topping up reservoirs and rivers downstream. In hard winters the reservoir has been known to have a thick covering of ice.

The rocks overlooking the **Chew Valley** have long been favoured

The author by the memorial cross above Ashway Gap

crags of the Manchester climbing fraternity, amongst them the late Don Whillans and Joe Brown. There are hundreds of routes laid down and as is always the case, the routes are given names that reflect either the difficulty of ascent or the state of mind of the person who first climbed the line. A perfect example is Appointment With Death (E9 6c).

Turn left across the dam and, where it changes direction going sharply to the right, take the footpath on the left signposted 'Public Footpath to Ashway Stone'. A series of cairns guides you north through the labyrinth of groughs and streams that lead from Dish Stone Moss onto **Dove Stone Moss** and brings you to a footbridge over the stream at **Ashway Gap**. Cross the bridge, the stream now on your left, and follow the footpath northwest until just after it connects with the path coming down from Dean Rocks. Here, turn north and follow the path across moorland keeping on the high path to eventually arrive at the **Ashway Stone**. Continue north along the path across the moor to the memorial cross above Ashway Gap.

The **memorial cross** above Ashway Gap is in memory of James Platt who came from a family of local industrialists and was MP for Oldham. The family had a shooting lodge built in the Gothic manor at Ashway Gap below, near to what is now Dove Stone Reservoir. James Platt died in a shooting accident on the moor above the house and the family placed this ornate cross in his memory. It is one of many structures placed high on the moors in the Dark Peak as memorials to some person or cause.

From the memorial cross proceed north along the footpath, the route turning northwest to drop down a steep slope and onto the edge of the spur at **Ashway Rocks**. Follow the footpath around the top of the spur eventually facing east at **Raven Stones Brow** where you will encounter towering rock formations known as the Trinnacle. After these outstanding rock pinnacles the path turns inward, southeast, and starts its descent into Birchen Clough and a fording place across the stream.

The Trinnacle above Raven Stones Brow

Birchen Clough is one of the most beautiful cloughs in the whole of the Dark Peak. The waters tumble down a series of waterfalls and cascades, a cacophony of musical notes to accompany the adventurous walker. The narrow path down the streambank does become flooded in times of heavy rain, making progress difficult – if not impossible – so care should be taken. There are two major steps down along the path, both passable with care, and these miniature gritstone crags add a little excitement to the descent.

Ford the stream and turn left to walk the narrow path downstream, passing many waterfalls on the way and making easy scrambles down a couple of sections where a little caution is required, to gain the path a few metres below. Eventually the stream turns sharp right where a suitable fording place exists that gives you access across a stone bridge with metal handrails to the reservoir track heading west beside Greenfield Brook.

Follow the well-made track down to **Yeoman Hey Reservoir**, and carry straight on down the track and take the footpath immediately on your left through a gate that leads down to the edge of the **Dove Stone Reservoir**. The waterside footpath eventually delivers you to the northern end of Dove Stone Reservoir, which you access across a small footbridge. Walk across the dam to return to the Dove Stone car park.

WALK 31

Binn Green to Great Dove Stone Rock

Start/Finish	Binn Green SE 017 044
Distance	6.5km (4 miles)
Ascent	381m
Time	2hrs
Terrain	Open moorland, footpaths and tracks
Map	OS 1:25000 Explorer OL1 Dark Peak
Parking	Binn Green car park SE 017 044

The big attraction of this route is the short walk to the top. In no time at all you can be sat high above Dove Stone Reservoir enjoying fantastic views from the cairn on Fox Stone. The descent by the reservoir cascade is very pleasant on a sunny summer's day. This is a nice morning or afternoon ramble especially in fine weather. The ascent is not too strenuous and there are plenty of opportunities to stop and take in the views. If so desired this walk can easily be made longer by descending via the Chew Road instead.

From the Binn Green car park take the footpath sign-posted 'Dove Stone' south down the steps and through trees to a gap in a stone wall with a gate beyond leading onto a tarmac lane. Once in the lane turn left and walk down towards **Yeoman Hey Reservoir** passing through a gate on the way. Go across the dam and at the end turn right onto a wide reservoir track heading south with Dove Stone Reservoir on your right. Pass through a gate alongside a cattle grid and after 20 metres follow the footpath on your left up the hillside to a stile, not visible

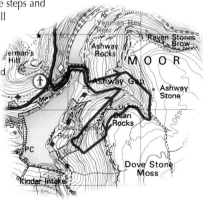

from the reservoir track, in a wire fence. Go over the stile to follow the footpath up the moorland using the Ashway Stone, the large boulder on the horizon, as your guide.

Below the Ashway Stone is **Ashway Gap**, the site of the Neo-Gothic mansion built by John Platt as a shooting lodge. His brother James was killed in a shooting accident a few hundred metres to the right of the boulder. A memorial cross was erected in his memory and now stands overlooking Dove Stone Reservoir. The house was demolished in 1981.

The longer walk via the Chew Valley road continues south along the edge path at this point.

Approaching the **Ashway Stone**, head right along a footpath taking you above the clough that leads down to Ashway Gap. Follow the footpath, fording the stream to reach the opposite side of the clough. Turn right and follow the edge-path past **Dean Rocks** and Great Dove Stone Rocks to arrive at the cairn on Fox Stone. ◀

Immediately before the cairn follow the footpath right, down the hillside, over a stile in a wire fence, to

Overlooking Dove Stone

Dove Stone Rocks

a grass track running left to right with a stone wall a few metres beyond, on Sunny Brow. Turn right and walk down the track, entering a tree plantation through a gap in a wall. Proceed along the woodland track to a stile. Do not go over the stile but take the track leading up through trees on the right and follow the fence line across broken ground to a stile which when crossed will give you access to the footbridge across the cascade bringing water down from the tunnel above to Dove Stone Reservoir below.

> The **tunnel** was constructed as a bypass for water running from Holme Clough to Ashway Gap and to placate mill owners who feared that their water supply would be interrupted with the construction of the dams.

After crossing the footbridge turn immediately left and follow the vehicle track alongside the cascade. At the bottom go through the gate and onto the reservoir track. Turn right along the track with **Dove Stone Reservoir** on your left and retrace your footsteps back to Binn Green car park and the end of the walk.

WALK 32

Cotton Famine Road

Start/Finish	Binn Green SE 017 044
Distance	12.5km (7½ miles)
Ascent	345m
Time	4hrs
Terrain	Open moorland, footpaths and tracks
Map	OS 1:25000 Explorer OL1 Dark Peak
Parking	Binn Green car park SE 017 044

Walkers interested in history and wildlife will find much to explore on this route. It takes you to a monument to the local villagers who fell in both World Wars, making for a sobering moment, and then across a moorland landscape that has been transformed from a barren sterile environment to one full of flowers and insects, birds and wildlife by the work of the Moors For The Future agency. Then on to one of the most spectacular and seldom-seen sights in the Dark Peak, the view from above of Birchen Clough at Saddleworth Moor.

From the Binn Green car park cross the A635 and go through the metal gate leading onto the Oldham Way. Follow the trail, a wide cart track between walls, for a distance of just over a kilometre until you reach a footpath running east to west across the trail. Take the waymarked trail heading north through the gateway on the right to cross a wooden stile and follow the footpath ascending first left and then right around the outskirts of the quarry to eventually arrive at the **Obelisk War Memorial**.

The **Obelisk**, a war memorial erected in 1923, can be viewed from all the villages that are named on the bronze plaques. The names of all those who perished in both World Wars are inscribed on the plaques.

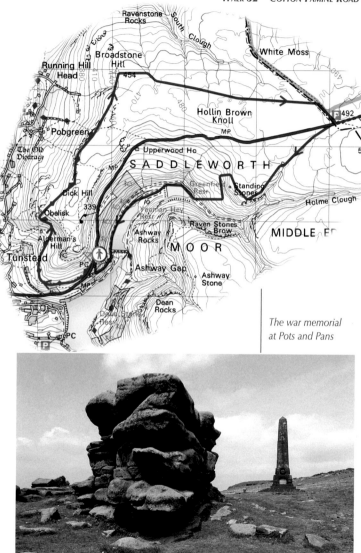

The war memorial
at Pots and Pans

The surrounding area is known as **Pots and Pans** due to the shape of the weathered gritstone formations. From the Obelisk vantage point you can also view the Oven Stones and the Sugar Loaf. Two quarries in the area were famous for producing bakestones, flat stones that could be placed in a fire and used to cook oatcakes, a local delicacy.

From the Obelisk go 60 metres directly east towards the Oven Stones and at the stone Oldham waymarker post at the end of an iron fence follow the path northeast over moorland and across a tumbledown stone wall to arrive at a stile by a metal farm gate. Step across the stile and proceed along the defined vehicle track for 500 metres up to the top of Sugar Loaf Hill. On reaching the top look carefully for a low waymark post sitting in front of a metal post on your left. Go left here heading north to Shaw Rocks, then continue straight ahead for 400 metres to reach a wire sheep fence running northeast. Go over a stile and follow the fence now on your right, along a wide and at times boggy track. Cross one more stile and keep on the same heading to finally reach the triangulation pillar on **Broadstone Hill**.

Go southeast from the triangulation pillar for 200 metres, working your way across open moorland, then go east for 270 metres to reach the remains of a stone cabin at the side of a wide cutting dug deep into the moor and running off into the northwest. This is the Cotton Famine Road.

Turn right along the Cotton Famine Road and follow it for 2.3km until you reach a stone-flagged path. Go right, along the path to a stile leading onto the **A635** road. Go right and across the road. Where the road sign and boundary stone for Saddleworth are situated go over the stile on the left onto the open moor. Follow the route of the road until reaching the beginning of Rimmon Pit Clough and go left to follow the course of the stream running down this clough until a wide manmade track running up to the remains of Rimmon Cottage on the left appears. Go right, up the track to the building remains

THE COTTON FAMINE ROAD

It is said that the Cotton Famine Road marks a dark period in the fortunes of the surrounding villages. Due to the American Civil War supplies of raw cotton were blockaded from reaching the mills, bringing production to a halt, which in turn put the mill workers out of work. No social support was available at that time and people began to starve. To alleviate the starvation local parishes put men, women and children to work on projects around the parish. The story goes that one of these was the Cotton Famine Road. This all falls apart when it is noted that the road first appeared on a map 20 years before the American Civil War began. However, it may well be that the road was built for the reasons the myth suggests as there were famines before the cotton embargo.

and step across the stream on the left that feeds into Rimmon Pit Clough, and subsequently follow the moor along the top edge of the clough to arrive at a spur of land above the junction of Holme Clough, Birchen Clough and Greenfield Brook.

Rimmon Cottage

From the spur go northwest to **Standing Stones** and 100 metres after passing the rocks, at a saddle below the rising hill to Adams Cross, go left down the moor and then work your way south for 200 metres traversing the hillside, then descend west down a southwest facing slope. Do not go too far right over the stream heading down the hillside. Exit onto the reservoir maintenance track heading down the valley at the head of **Greenfield Reservoir**. Follow the track to **Yeoman Hey Reservoir dam** and carry straight on up the lane going through a wooden gate on the right that leads onto a woodland path on the right that returns you to Binn Green car park and the end of the walk.

Shining Tor (Walk 33)

It may seem strange to include an area that is on the other side of Buxton and practically surrounded by White Peak limestone in a book of walks in the Dark Peak, but it is a marvellous example of how, hundreds of millions of years ago, the Dark Peak was formed through sedimentation, movement and erosion. The gritstone and peat stand up in the midst of all that white limestone, islands in a sea of green pasture and white rock. The walking is more pastoral here and involves much more farmland than in the rest of the Dark Peak. This makes the walks all the more enticing because when you do come upon the gritstone and the peat it is such a contrast.

Ramsden Rocks, Hen Cloud and the Roaches are an assault on the senses. They protrude from the landscape, proclaiming their existence. Stand upon them and you are greeted with a view across a plain punctuated with steep hills and, on the horizon, the faint shimmering outline of the Welsh mountains. It is unexpected. As is Lud's Church. There is nothing else like it in the Dark Peak. The approach to this natural cleft, down through a dark and dank woodland path with wet gritstone boulders, is a portent of what is to come. Bedecked in mosses and ferns, it is full of intrigue and myth. Shutlingsloe and Shining Tor are the perfect viewpoints across a flat plain out to Wales. Look closely and you may see the Lovell Telescope at Jodrell Bank rotating, seeking out some unseen civilisation billions of miles away.

WALK 33
Goyt Valley to Shining Tor

Start/Finish	Errwood Reservoir car park SK 013 756
Distance	15km (9 miles)
Ascent	555m
Time	5hrs
Terrain	Open moorland, footpaths and forest tracks
Map	OS 1:25000 Explorer OL24 White Peak
Parking	Errwood Reservoir car park SK 013 756

The Goyt Valley is a little, hidden secret just outside Buxton. In summer the valley is resplendent with rhododendron flowers that add a wonderful backdrop and a heavy scent, as one climbs out of the valley and up onto Shining Tor. The walk from Shining Tor to Windgather Rocks gives a walker the opportunity to really stretch the legs along a long moorland ridge, something that is not too common in the Dark Peak. The forest walk back to Errwood Reservoir is an unexpected delight, a feast of birdlife, trees and fungi.

From the car park at the western end of Errwood Reservoir dam take the reservoir road through the gates, southwest, crossing the bridge over Shooter's Clough and turning into the car park on the southern side of the bridge. Go up the steps on the western edge of the car park and take the waymarked footpath passing through a gap in a low wall and a metal barrier across the path onto the wide trail with a stream initially on your right and then left. At the signpost for **Errwood Hall** take the track on the right that doubles back uphill to steps leading up to the remains of the building.

The Grimshawe family built **Errwood Hall**, high on the valley slopes above Goyt Bridge, in the mid 1800s. They were manufacturers and built the house in order to escape the filth and grime

Errwood Hall

of industrial Lancashire. By the 1930s the family was reduced to just two daughters, both married but without children. When they died Stockport Corporation purchased the estate for the construction of two reservoirs.

Take the footpath directly opposite the wall with four arches and follow it through ornate gateposts to rejoin the main forest trail. Where the trail meets open ground by a fingerpost follow the footpath left, signposted 'Stakeside'. Follow the footpath up the narrow clough keeping the stream on your left until the footpath fords the stream and joins a track that zig zags uphill to a wooden gate giving access onto open moorland.

Go through the gate turning right to proceed along a moorland path with the drystone wall on your right until you reach a gate in the wall opposite a finger post pointing the way to **Shining Tor**. Cross the wall via the gate and walk up the clearly defined footpath to the triangulation pillar.

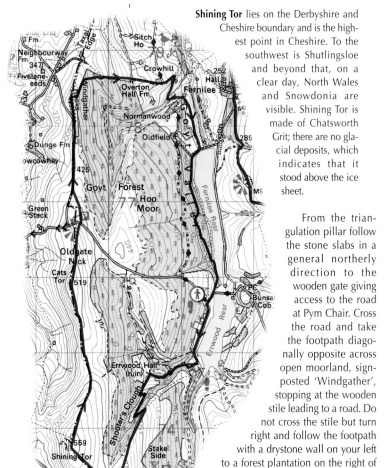

Shining Tor lies on the Derbyshire and Cheshire boundary and is the highest point in Cheshire. To the southwest is Shutlingsloe and beyond that, on a clear day, North Wales and Snowdonia are visible. Shining Tor is made of Chatsworth Grit; there are no glacial deposits, which indicates that it stood above the ice sheet.

From the triangulation pillar follow the stone slabs in a general northerly direction to the wooden gate giving access to the road at Pym Chair. Cross the road and take the footpath diagonally opposite across open moorland, signposted 'Windgather', stopping at the wooden stile leading to a road. Do not cross the stile but turn right and follow the footpath with a drystone wall on your left to a forest plantation on the right of the path. Go through the wooden gate across the footpath and proceed up onto the top of **Windgather Rocks**.

Apart from the excitement of seeing people climbing on **Windgather Rocks** there is

Climbers on Windgather Rocks

much to be learned from the geology of the area. The rocks are of Chatsworth Grit laid down some 300 million years ago when the area was positioned over the equator and it became a vast river delta. The layering of the rock is indicative of silt build-up and the movement of the river delta over millions of years which produced the distinctive formations, often crossing to form layers in different directions.

Walk along the top of the gritstone escarpment and where a gap appears in a drystone wall across your direction of travel take the footpath through the wooden gate down to the right in front of the wall and follow the wall line along to reach a wooden stile with a waymark sign pointing right into the forest. Cross the stile and follow the footpath right, down through the forest to a wooden footbridge that should be crossed and follow the path uphill to a ladder stile by a wall.

Goyt Valley

Cross the ladder stile and turn right to follow a footpath signed for Overton Hall, directly east down open moorland to a road. Cross the road and proceed across a cattle grid and down a tarmac track, the track switching back to descend to a metal gate just prior to where the tarmac ends and a stone track begins. Go through the gate and follow the stone track down to cross a stream then turn left uphill through two wooden gates keeping to the track until you reach the western end of **Fernilee Reservoir dam**.

Go through the wooden gate and then right across a car park onto a tarmac lane. Take a left at the fingerpost to enter woodland through a wooden gate heading for Errwood Reservoir. Proceed through the woodland, keeping to the waymark signs for the Woodland Walk and crossing two wooden bridges to eventually join the reservoir track that returns you to **Errwood Reservoir car park**.

WALK 34
Derbyshire Bridge to Shutlingsloe

Start/Finish	Derbyshire Bridge Ranger Centre SK 018 715
Distance	20km (12½ miles)
Ascent	848m
Time	7hrs
Terrain	Open moorland, footpaths and forest tracks
Map	OS 1:25000 Explorer OL24 White Peak
Parking	Derbyshire Bridge Ranger Centre SK 018 715

The walk starts from the Peak District National Park Ranger Centre at Derbyshire Bridge, on the boundary of Derbyshire and Cheshire. Initially the walk crosses open moorland and several roads until it begins its descent towards the beautiful Three Shire Heads and the River Dane at Panniers Pool. From there the walk heads over to Hollinsclough and probably the grandest post office in the country, before striking out for the ascent of Shutlingsloe and the reward of the views across the Cheshire Plains. A great deal of beautiful scenery makes this a rewarding walk.

From Derbyshire Bridge car park take the footpath south-east across open moorland to a wooden gate leading onto a stone track. Go left along the track to cross the **A54** road and head right, to a wooden gate leading to open moorland. Follow the grass track south, across **Axe Edge Moor**, passing a fenced-off mine on the right, then immediately after follow the track left to meet a stone track. Walk right, along its length to meet a minor road at Dane Head. Go through the wooden gate, then right, down the road and take the first footpath left on the opposite side marked by a small waymark post. Follow this trail over a small ford to cross a stone stile in a wall, and walk diagonally across a field eventually meeting a vehicle track. Turn right, along the track, go over a cattle grid and bear

Panniers Pool and packhorse bridge at Three Shire Heads

left where the track meets a second going up to a farm.

Note the **coal seam** on the left of the track. Part of the geological make-up of the area, the coal is the remains of trees and plantlife that thrived in the river delta when this area was over the equator. The coal measures, along with shale and mudstone, lie in layers within the gritstone that covers the Dark Peak.

Continue along the track and take the first right down towards Black Clough Farm, turning right by the gate and following the waymarked footpath up the hillside to **Black Clough Farm**. At the farm go over the unusual wooden stile, cross a field to go over a second stile then walk right, along the fence line, to follow the indistinct track down the hillside with the stream on the right to reach a stile leading to a junction of roads and footpaths. Go over the wooden stile and take the right

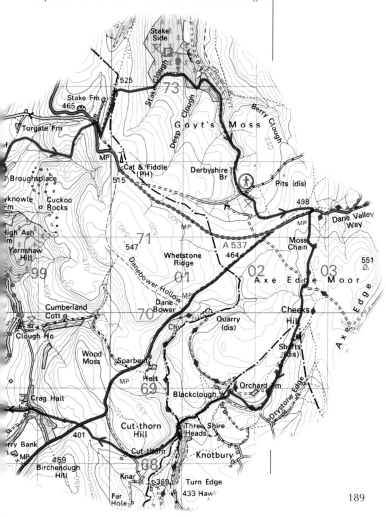

189

hand footpath of two immediately ahead, heading south-west, and follow this through a metal gate to pass a small packhorse bridge on the left. Go right following the track down to a packhorse bridge and Panniers Pool below **Three Shire Heads**.

> **Three Shire Heads** is the name of the hill, not the bridge, that sits at the meeting-point of the counties of Derbyshire, Cheshire and Staffordshire. The bridge below is on an old packhorse route used to carry salt from Cheshire, coal from Axe Edge and silk from Hollinsclough, among other goods. The pool below the bridge is Panniers Pool, where the packhorse trains – with panniers loaded – would have drunk.

Cross the bridge and follow the track left around the hillside to **Cut-thorn**. Go right for a few metres and then take the footpath left through the gate and across fields bearing right to a stone stile with a wooden stile a couple of metres beyond. Go over both and follow the wooden

The Old Post Office, Wildboarclough

boardwalks to a farm gate in a wall. Go through the gate and follow the footpath past a small barn on the left to a wall by the forest plantation. Proceed through a gate into the plantation following the woodland path down to a road. Turn right and walk down the road, past Crag Mill and the wonderful Old Post Office on the right to the road junction at **Wildboarclough**. ▶

Go left along the road a few metres and at a layby walk across the road and turn right up the tarmac lane towards Shutlingsloe. Follow the yellow waymark signs up the lane then bear left before the farm to ascend the hillside via a footbridge and stile. Keep to the left hand path that winds its way up the left side of Shutlingsloe, finally ending at the top southern end. The **triangulation pillar** is at the northern end and boasts fine views across the Cheshire Plain.

> **Shutlingsloe**, Shutlings Hlaw, Shutlings Hill in present day terms is known locally as the Matterhorn of Cheshire. From the summit the hills of North Wales can be viewed, as well as the giant radio telescope at Jodrell Bank.

Take the northwest stone path down from the summit. ▶ Go over the strange stile and gate combination to reach a metal kissing gate on the left. Go through the gate, you do not have to kiss, and follow the stone footpath across the moor to a wooden gate giving access into **Macclesfield Forest**. After going through the gate turn immediately right and follow the footpath down to join the main forest track. Go right, along the track until it meets with a public road at a farm gate. Turn right, down the road and at the next junction go left then take the first footpath on the right up a tarmac lane to **Broughsplace**.

Pass to the left of the buildings and take the wooden gate on the left through trees to a wooden footbridge across a stream. At the other side of the bridge turn right along the line of the wall and follow the waymark signs left to an abandoned farmstead, bearing right by what remains of the farm building, then across fields to a gate

---

The Old Post Office was built in the early 19th century as offices for Crag Works, later becoming a post office and postmaster's house.

Take care descending, as it is very steep and can be slippery in wet weather.

in a drystone wall. Go through the gate and continue ahead until you see the signs for the concessionary footpath, before you reach the farm buildings. Follow the waymark posts right, down the hillside to a metal gate. Go through this gate and across the field still following the waymark posts to a stone stile leading up Chest Hollow.

Follow the footpath ahead and when it starts to turn left uphill just past a sheepfold below on the right, continue following it to reach a wooden stile giving access onto the A537. Go straight across the road and take the driveway left to a footpath sign. Follow the sign right, up to a track coming from the **Cat and Fiddle public house**. Turn left along the track, through a gate and continue until you reach a footpath sign on the right. Go over the stile and descend towards Goytsclough Quarry. Where the footpath meets a metal gate bear right along a wire fence to a wooden stile. Cross this and continue your descent through trees to cross a wooden footbridge, then follow the fingerposts indicating Derbyshire Bridge. Leave the woodland at a wooden gate and go right following the treeline across open ground to meet the road going up to Derbyshire Bridge. Head right, up the road to eventually arrive back at **Derbyshire Bridge**.

WALK 35
The Roaches

Start/Finish	Gradbach car park SJ 998 662
Distance	16km (10 miles)
Ascent	601m
Time	5hrs
Terrain	Open moorland, footpaths and forest tracks
Map	OS 1:25000 Explorer OL24 White Peak
Parking	Gradbach car park SJ 998 662

A line of gritstone projects out of the moorland and points to the eastern edge of the Dark Peak, west to the mountain ranges of Wales and south across flat plains to the hills of Shropshire. This is the last hurrah of the gritstone girdle that holds within it the limestone of the White Peak. To stand on Hen Cloud of an evening and watch the sun set across the vast plain is a spine-tingling moment. Combine this with the secretive and alluring Lud's Church, with all the myths and legends that go along with this eerie place, and you have a fitting finale to a tour of the Dark Peak.

From Gradbach car park follow the narrow lane west to a fork at Gradbach House Farm. Take the right fork and follow the track to a gate on the left leading into a farmyard immediately before a cottage. Go through the gate into the farmyard and along the right hand track past a stone reclamation yard to a metal gate across a track heading south. Go through the gate and continue along the farm track across fields to a second metal gate. Go through the second gate and then immediately left through a field gate into farm pasture along a concessionary access, turning immediately right to follow the boundary line along on the right. Eventually the wire fence boundary becomes a drystone wall. The footpath crosses fields and tumbledown walls to reach a gate at Cloughhead. Go through the wooden gate and right, along the path with a wall on the right, uphill to a second wooden gate that leads to a minor road.

At the junction with the road take the tarmac farm track right, through a gate to Moss End Farm. Do not enter the farm, but take the left hand waymarked footpath down through a gate to a signpost indicating to go left for Blackbank. Take this path left crossing first a stone and then a wooden stile, to a farm track leading to **Goldsitch House**, by a PNFS signpost. Go straight on across the field to a gate giving access to a farm track. Go right, down the track and then follow the fingerpost left over a stone bridge to step over a steel stile.

Ramshaw Rocks

Follow a footpath around the perimeter of farm buildings over a wooden stile and then along a wall to a further stile and then through a gate to gain the footpath crossing a field.

Follow the line of a tumbledown wall to arrive at a wooden footbridge and stile leading onto a road. Turn right, along the road and take the footpath over a wall to the left of a metal farm gate to **Hazel Barrow**. On reaching the farm go left up a concrete drive between two stone buildings to a road. Go left along the road and at the junction bear right to take the signposted footpath right, through two gates and a stile and a final steep ascent before turning right, along a fence line to reach **Ramshaw Rocks**.

Ramshaw Rocks, along with the Hen Cloud and the Roaches, were formed around 320 million years ago from sands deposited along a delta. The grit-stone that was produced in this part of the Dark Peak, seen today in the area's outcrops of freestone,

195

is capable of being worked in any direction and is therefore favoured by masons. It also makes for excellent climbing venues.

Follow the path along the top of Ramshaw Rocks, passing through two wooden gates to descend to a road. Turn left and follow the road around a tight left hand bend and just after the bend take the footpath right, down across moorland to a lane leading to a farm. Turn right, along the lane and then bear left at the fork and go through the gate leading into a field on the left to follow the waymarked concessionary path around the farm perimeter at **Naychurch**. Go across the drive on the western side of the farm buildings and through a gap in the wall leading to a grass footpath heading north downhill.

At the bottom of the footpath, before reaching the house, turn sharp left to continue down the footpath to ford a small stream. Go over a wooden stile then ascend around a hillside to head northwest over fields to **Well Farm**. At the first farm building take the footpath immediately left down to a stream. Cross the stream and enter access land on Hen Cloud bearing left uphill to reach a footpath running northwest around the hillside to a gate in the wall giving access to the Roaches. Do not go through the gate but turn left up the stone paved footpath to the top of **Hen Cloud**. ◄

Peregrine falcons have started to use the rock face for nesting. When this happens the top of Hen Cloud is cordoned off to ensure the birds are not disturbed.

Retrace your steps to the wall and go through the gate turning left to follow the footpath to the Don Whillans Memorial Hut, named Rockhall on the OS map. Go up the footpath on the left of the perimeter wall of the building to reach stone steps that will take you up onto a woodland trail leading along the bottom of the Roaches' face. Go left and follow the trail until it intersects with a footpath rising from below. Turn right and follow the stone path up onto the top of **the Roaches**. Turn left and follow the footpath along the Roaches heading in a northerly direction and passing the Doxey Pool and the **triangulation pillar** on the way.

The natural cleft of Lud's Church

The Roaches is a magical place. The views alone make it special. A mermaid is said to inhabit the Doxey Pool and the moors surrounding the area are home to the famous wallabies (descendants of the original five that escaped from a private zoo during World War Two), although there has been no confirmed sighting for many years.

Eventually the path meets a road signposted 'Gradbach'; turn right, down the road and proceed to a very slim gap in a wall on the left. Go through the gap and follow the wall into woodland. Here a signpost by a large tree points left to Lud's Church. Follow this along a forest trail to a further signpost pointing left up to a third

197

signpost which tells you to go right, to Lud's Church. On reaching the chasm go to the left of the wooden railings and then descend where indicated into the abyss. Proceed along the floor of **Lud's Church** to exit by stone steps on the other side.

> **Lud's Church** is shrouded in myth and legend. It is said to have connections to Sir Gawain and the Green Knight. It was reputed to have been used by the Lollards for secret religious services when they were being persecuted. It is also said that the men of Flash Village used the chasm to clip coins in secrecy, the village giving its name to the term 'flash money'.

Turn left along the forest path to a signpost indicating that Gradbach lies to the right. Turn right, down the forest trail to a signpost taking you left down a slope to a large tree. Go right, by the tree and follow the signpost across a wooden bridge and through a gate to a footpath rising up by a wall to cross a stile on the left. Go left down a track through a gap in a wall on the right, then follow the wall left to a wooden gate leading to Gradbach Mill. Enter the mill yard and walk to the right of the mill up the tarmac drive to the road. Turn left down the road and return to **Gradbach car park** and the end of the walk.

LONG DAY WALKS

The Edale Horseshoe takes you right around the Vale of Edale (Walk 39)

Long days in the Dark Peak mean sunrises upon the high moors and sunsets sat on gritstone edges looking out over the dramatic landscape. Each walk is based around the three main aspects of the Dark Peak: gritstone edges, high moorland and deep valleys. These walks offer the very best of the landscape along with an experience of the solitude of moorland walking and a geological view of the area. The walker is free to marvel at the beauty of a landscape so close and yet so far away from the people in the valleys below. These route descriptions are not detailed directions. Rather they are a general overview of the principal points along the route, and it is of course possible to deviate from the route to take in a specific feature.

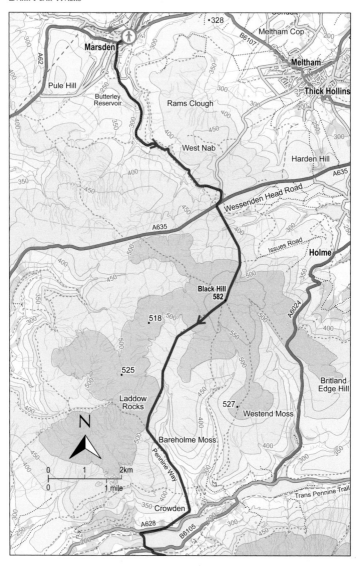

WALK 36

Marsden to Edale

Start	Marsden SE 049 115
Finish	Edale SK 123 857
Distance	40km (25 miles)
Ascent	1465m
Time	13hrs
Terrain	Open moorland, footpaths and exposed edges
Map	OS 1:25000 Explorer OL1 Dark Peak
Public transport	No direct public transport routes link the start and finish, but there is a bus-stop and station in both Marsden and Edale
Parking	Marsden station SE 048 118

This outline of the classic full day's walk across the Dark Peak moors takes some beating for a sense of achievement. It is long, it is hard, and it is exhausting: what more could a lover of the high moorlands want? Starting from Marsden and following the Pennine Way in parts back to Edale, the walk takes in every one of the iconic moorlands: Black Hill, Bleaklow and Kinder Scout. A long day, yes, but one with so much to offer: wild moorland, solitude, tough peat groughs, gritstone edges, wide open skies and tumbling streams. Finish the walk in Edale with a pint at the Old Nags Head pub and then a train home.

Setting off from the **Marsden** information centre walk southeast down Peel Street to the junction with the A62 and turn right down the road, then left at the next junction down Fall Lane, signposted 'Butterley Reservoir and Spillway'. At the small roundabout go up Binn Road and take the cobbled lane between two towering mill buildings. Take the flight of steps leading up by the reservoir slipway. At the top walk straight on with a stone wall on your right and join the Kirklees Way and public bridleway, going directly south along the edges of both

map continues on page 202

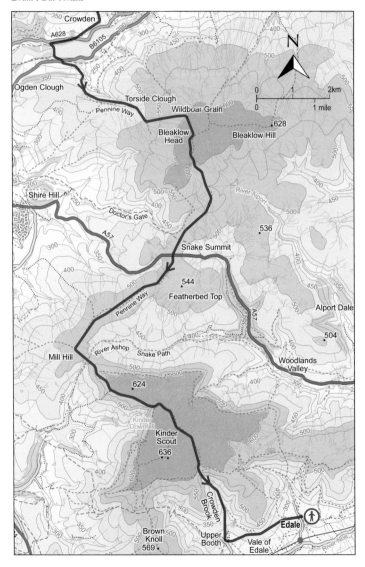

Butterley Reservoir and Blakeley Reservoir. As the trail leaves the second reservoir it meets the Pennine Way, which you now follow. Keep straight on along the track to **Wessenden Head Road**.

Go through the gate and right, down the road to its junction with the **A635**, cross the road and turn right and walk for 150 metres, then take the Pennine Way footpath left to **Black Hill**. From the triangulation pillar take the paved footpath southwest down the hill towards Red Ratcher, following the stream down the valley floor before ascending to **Laddow Rocks**. Follow the edge path southwest then southeast to meet a farm track rising from **Crowden**. Turn right along the track heading west with the **A628** running parallel, until the path meets and crosses the road and drops down through woodland to cross Torside Reservoir. Turn left at the end of the dam and cross a road right to pick up the **Pennine Way** footpath heading for Reaps. Carry on down the track until you follow the Pennine Way right, up **Torside Clough**.

Across the high moors from Marsden to Edale

Turn left at **Wildboar Grain** and trace the stream up to **Bleaklow Head**.

From Bleaklow Head follow the stone Pennine Way posts initially southwest and then south to Hern Clough, then make sure you stay on the Pennine Way as it turns first southeast then southwest to reach **Snake Summit** on the **A57**.

Go straight across the A57 and continue on the stone slabs of the Pennine Way heading for **Mill Hill**, where you turn left to ascend to the Kinder Plateau and **Kinder Scout**. Follow the edge path to **Kinder Downfall** and then turn left along the footpath following the River Kinder upstream, passing the stones known as the Kinder Gates and crossing the watershed of Edale Moor to meet the southern edge path at **Crowden Brook**. Descend Crowden Brook, following the footpath down to **Upper Booth**. From Upper Booth join the Pennine Way again heading east into **Edale** and the Old Nags Head pub.

WALK 37
Langsett to Edale

Start	Langsett Barn SE 211 004
Finish	Edale SK 123 857
Distance	25km (15½ miles)
Ascent	960m
Time	8hrs
Terrain	Open moorland, footpaths and tracks
Map	OS 1:25000 Explorer OL1 Dark Peak
Public transport	No direct public transport routes link the start and finish, but there is a bus-stop at Langsett Barn and a bus-stop and station in Edale
Parking	Langsett Barn SE 211 004

The outline of this walk follows part of the old route that jaggers (a person who leads a team of packhorses) used to bring livestock to Penistone market. It crosses several valleys using natural lines. Some of the crossing points no longer exist today so alternative routes have been used. The route starts at Langsett, the beginning of the first packhorse bridleway, Cut Gate, which crosses the watershed into the Derwent Valley and then climbs up and descends into the Woodlands Valley to then ascend to Hope Cross, an ancient crossroads. It then follows the old line along the Vale of Edale to the vaccaries or booths surrounding Edale.

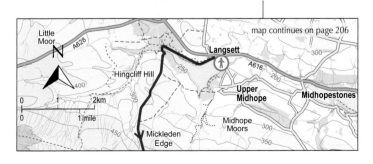

map continues on page 206

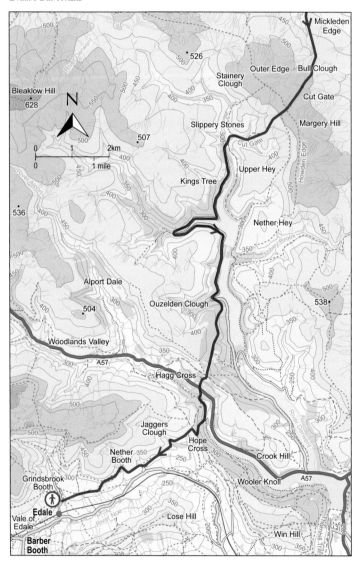

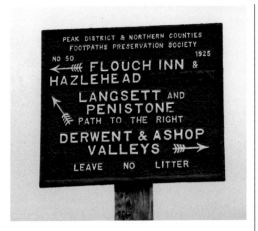

Langsett to Edale has been a route over the moors for centuries

From Langsett Barn car park take the woodland footpath to the River Don where it flows into **Langsett Reservoir**. Go through the gate leading up onto the moors and follow the Cut Gate bridleway all the way into the Upper Derwent Valley, passing the large cairn on Howden Edge and finishing at Slippery Stones on the River Derwent. Cross the old packhorse bridge. ▶ Follow the trail through woodland to the road head at **Kings Tree** and continue down the road, passing Howden Dam and through Birchinlee Village, the camp built for workers on the dam construction.

This used to be situated further down the valley in Derwent Village, which was submerged when the valley was flooded.

After the road switches back at **Ouzelden Clough** take the bridleway on the right up through trees to **Hagg Cross** then descend to cross the **A57** and carry on down to the River Ashop at Haggwater Bridge. Cross the bridge and ascend through trees to Hope Cross, then turn right along the old Roman road and before going through a metal gate turn left along the bridleway to **Jaggers Clough** and on to Clough Farm. Go right here and follow the footpath up across Lady Booth Brook and past the Edale YHA, following the path across fields to Ollerbrook Booth then on into **Grindsbrook Booth** and finally left down the road to **Edale**.

WALK 38
Gritstone edges

Start	Fairholmes Visitor Centre SK 172 893
Finish	Baslow SK 253 722
Distance	45km (28 miles)
Ascent	1200m
Time	13hrs
Terrain	Open moorland, footpaths and tracks
Map	OS 1:25000 Explorer OL1 Dark Peak; OS 1:25000 Explorer OL24 White Peak
Public transport	No direct public transport routes link the start and finish, but there is a bus-stop at both Fairholmes and Baslow
Parking	Fairholmes car park, located by the visitor centre, SK 172 893

Hundreds of millions of years have provided us with this superb walk along the Derwent Valley which links nine gritstone edges, offering high-level views across the valley that was gouged out by the River Derwent. All of the edges are famous for climbing and bouldering, with thousands of routes established over the many years they have been frequented. But access to one edge, Bamford Edge, has only just been made available thanks to the Countryside and Rights of Way (CRoW) Act 2000. Before the act, one needed express permission of the owners. This is a spectacular walk at any time of year.

From Fairholmes Visitor Centre in the Upper Derwent Valley follow Derwent Lane to where it meets the East Track going up the eastern side of Upper Derwent Reservoir. Walk up the East Track to Walker's Clough on the right and ascend the footpath crossing wall-stiles to Green Sitches and pick up the path that takes you on to Lost Lad. Go southeast from Lost Lad to Back Tor and then follow the wide trail south along **Derwent Edge** with its collection of gritstone boulders including the Salt Cellar

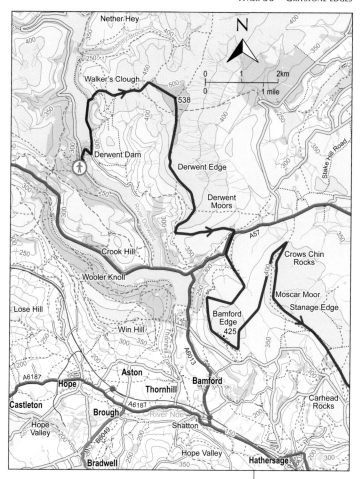

and the Cakes of Bread, to Whinstone Lee Tor. Turn left down the bridleway to Cutthroat Bridge then cross the **A57** to ascend Jarvis Clough onto Bamford Moor, bearing right at the Glory Stones to reach **Bamford Edge**.

map continues on page 210

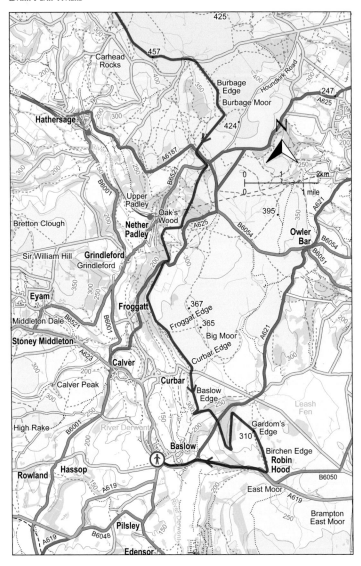

Follow the footpath southeast to the quarry at the end of the edge then turn north and follow the public footpath to **Crows Chin Rocks**. Go right, onto the footpath below the edge and where the quarry starts at Stanage End ascend the footpath onto the top of **Stanage Edge** and follow it south to High Neb then southeast to Upper Burbage Bridge. Cross the road and walk along **Burbage Moor** above Burbage Rocks arriving at Burbage Bridge on the **A6187**.

Cross the road to enter the Longshaw Estate and walk to Longshaw Lodge, then on through the estate southwest along a track to where it is intersected by a footpath running east to west. Head right, down the path and follow it through **Oak's Wood** and then Hay Wood to the **A625**. Walk right 50 metres to a gate on the opposite side of the road and enter the woods leading to **Froggatt Edge**. Continue on along the edge footpath south then southeast onto **Curbar Edge**. At Curbar Gap cross the road and walk south along **Baslow Edge** to Wellington's Monument where you turn right, down to a junction of four footpaths. Take the path immediately left heading practically northeast down a steep slope with a wall on the right to descend to the right of two houses then cross the A621 to the footpath directly opposite.

Follow the footpath up through woodland, crossing a wall, to reach **Gardom's Edge**. Go north along the edge and where the wall on the right finishes head right, through woodland and across the moor to ascend to the triangulation pillar on **Birchen Edge**. Turn right, passing Nelson's Monument and the Three Ships and follow the path south along the edge, dropping down the face at the end onto a forest track. Go right, along the track to the road, turn right and follow the road down to the **A619** and on to **Baslow** where public transport is available.

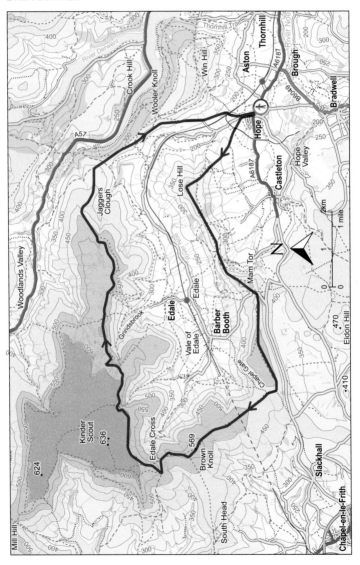

WALK 39
Edale Horseshoe

Start/Finish	Hope SK 172 834
Distance	28km (17½ miles)
Ascent	810m
Time	8hrs
Terrain	Open moorland, footpaths and tracks
Map	OS 1:25000 Explorer OL1 Dark Peak
Parking	Hope SK171 835

This walk follows the outline of the Vale of Edale on a southeast to northeast axis, starting and finishing in Hope. From the valley floor the walk quickly ascends onto the Great Ridge at Lose Hill, following it to Mam Tor and onto Lord's Seat and Rushup Edge before turning to Brown Knoll and then on via Edale Cross to Kinder Scout. It then turns back northeast along the southern edge of Kinder Scout before descending back into Hope via the old Roman Road from Hope Cross. The route gives magnificent views not only across the Vale of Edale, but east up the Derwent Valley and south across the White Peak.

From the church in Hope walk down Edale Road and take the second road left and then the footpath right, across an old railway line and fields to Losehill Farm. Follow the path behind the farm to join the footpath up to the summit of **Lose Hill**. From the summit go southwest along the Great Ridge to **Mam Tor** and descend to the road, crossing over to take the footpath directly opposite. Follow this keeping the boundary on the left past Lord's Seat to descend to a walled lane.

Turn right up **Chapel Gate** for 300 metres and take the concessionary footpath left up the ridgeline to **Brown Knoll**. Go past the triangulation pillar and turn right to follow a fence to join a bridleway where you turn left for **Edale Cross**. Go through the gate at the right of the cross and up through Swine's Back then bear right to join the Kinder Plateau edge path heading northeast then generally east until reaching **Grindsbrook**. Here the path turns north then back south again before continuing east to reach Crookstone Out Moor where it descends Crookstone Hill to join the bridleway to Hope Cross. Turn right to Hope Cross and carry on past it along the Roman road down the hillside to Fullwood Stile Farm. Where the road turns sharp right take the footpath straight ahead to pass under the railway line and rejoin Edale Road turning left back into **Hope**.

WALK 40

Kinder Scout skyline

Start/Finish	Birchin Clough SK 109 914
Distance	31km (19½ miles)
Ascent	1010m
Time	10hrs
Terrain	Open moorland, footpaths and tracks
Map	OS 1:25000 Explorer OL1 Dark Peak
Parking	Birchin Clough SK 109 914

The beauty of the Kinder Scout skyline walk is that you can start it from anywhere, as there are so many excellent ways onto the plateau. Many people look at the map and think that it will not take long to complete but it is deceptive, as there are many twists and turns and it is surprisingly easy to stray off the path and find yourself in the middle of the plateau totally lost. There are frequent calls for Mountain Rescue to find people lost on Kinder Scout and it can be disorientating in good weather as well as bad. Close attention to the chosen route will mitigate any problems and prevent that long walk back from descending into the wrong valley. The views are spectacular as you get a 360-degree panorama of the Dark Peak.

From Birchin Clough car park cross the **A57** and descend the footpath through woodland to Ashop Clough. Cross the footbridge and begin walking up the clough until you find a suitable fording place to cross the **River Ashop** below Saukin Ridge to reach the footpath on the other bank below Rough Bank. Turn left down the path and follow the river downstream to a wall where the river is joined by Fair Brook. Turn right and follow the brook up to the edge of the Kinder Plateau.

At the top turn right, north, and follow the edge path round to Fairbrook Naze and a superb vantage point over to the Upper Derwent moors. Continue along the path west to eventually cross a stile and drop down to

A short cut across Kinder Scout exists from here, taking the footpath east then south through the Kinder Gates and on to Crowden Brook.

the edge path now running south. Pass through two gates along Sandy Heys to arrive at Kinder Downfall. ◄ Cross Kinder Downfall and follow the path southwest to the triangulation pillar at Kinder Low. From the pillar, walk southeast over the summit of **Kinder Scout** to the southern edge path, turning left to reach Noe Stool. Proceed east along the edge path passing Pym Chair and Crowden Tower until Grindsbrook, where you head inland north for 400 metres then south again to regain the eastern path onto Ringing Roger.

Continue east past the Druid's Stone and on northeast to the spur that forms Crookstone Knoll. Walk west to where Blackden Brook falls from the Kinder Plateau

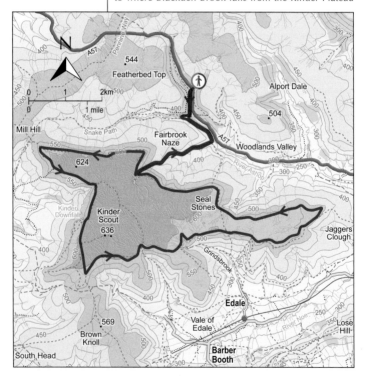

down into the **Woodlands Valley** below and then go north to Seal Stones and finally turning west along Seal Edge to return to Fair Brook and the descent back into the valley and return via the same route to Birchin Clough car park.

The Kinder skyline: a major challenge at anytime of year

APPENDIX A
Route summary table

Walk		Start/Finish	Distance	Time	Page
1	Chatsworth to Birchen Edge	Chatsworth House SK 259 702	17.5km (11 miles)	5hrs	28
2	Longshaw Estate and the gritstone edges	Longshaw Lodge SK 264 799	14km (9 miles)	4hrs	34
3	Fox House to Big Moor	Fox House Inn SK 267 802	18km (11 miles)	5hrs	38
4	Fox House to Stanedge Pole	Fox House Inn SK 267 802	16km (10 miles)	5hrs	42
5	Grindleford to Higger Tor	Grindleford Station SK 251 787	10km (6 miles)	3hrs	48
6	Hathersage to Stanage Edge	Hathersage bus shelter SK 230 815	8.5km (5 miles)	3hrs	54
7	Wyming Brook to Stanage Edge	Redmires Reservoirs car park SK 256 856	18km (11 miles)	6hrs	58
8	Bamford Moor	Heatherdene car park SK 202 858	12.5km (7½ miles)	4hrs	64
9	Win Hill to Hope Cross	Heatherdene car park SK 202 858	12.5km (7½ miles)	4hrs	69
10	Kings Tree to Shepherds Meeting Stones	Kings Tree, Upper Derwent Valley, SK 167 983	17km (10½ miles)	5hrs	73
11	Westend and Bleaklow Stones	Westend, Upper Derwent Valley, SK 154 927	16.5km (10 miles)	5hrs	78
12	Derwent Edge	Fairholmes Visitor Centre SK 172 893	16km (10 miles)	5hrs	82
13	Alport Castles and the Woodlands Valley	Fairholmes Visitor Centre SK 172 893	12.5km (7½ miles)	4hrs	86
14	Margery Hill to Back Tor	Fairholmes Visitor Centre SK 172 893	21km (13 miles)	7hrs	91
15	Low Bradfield and Dale Dyke	Low Bradfield car park SK 262 920	10km (6 miles)	3hrs	95
16	Langsett to Howden Edge	Langsett Barn SE 211 004	15.5km (10 miles)	5hrs	99
17	Langsett to Pike Lowe	Langsett Barn SE 211 004	11km (7 miles)	4hrs	103
18	Torside to Bleaklow Head	Torside car park SK 068 983	16.5km (10 miles)	6hrs	107
19	Wildboar Clough to Lawrence Edge	Torside car park SK 068 983	9.5km (6 miles)	4hrs	111
20	Old Glossop to Bleaklow Head	Shepley Street, Old Glossop, SK 045 948	13km (8 miles)	4hrs	115

Walk		Start/Finish	Distance	Time	Page
21	Kinder Scout Northern Edge	Birchen Clough car park, A57, SK 109 914	22km (14 miles)	7hrs	119
22	Kinder Scout Western Edge	Bowden Bridge car park, Hayfield, SK 048 869	13.5km (8 miles)	5hrs	124
23	Kinder Scout	Edale car park SK 123 853	16km (10 miles)	5hrs	130
24	Kinder Scout Southern Edge	Edale car park SK 123 853	13km (8 miles)	5hrs	136
25	The Great Ridge	Castleton, National Park Visitor Centre, SK 149 829	12km (7½ miles)	4hrs	140
26	Dunford Bridge to Ramsden Clough	Dunford Bridge SE 158 023	18.5km (11½ miles)	6hrs	146
27	Crowden Horseshoe	Crowden car park SK 072 992	16km (10 miles)	5hrs	151
28	Crowden to Chew Valley	Crowden car park SK 072 992	16km (10 miles)	5hrs	156
29	Marsden to Black Hill	Marsden SE 049 115	22km (13½ miles)	7hrs	161
30	Alphin Pike to Birchen Clough	Dove Stone Reservoir SE 013 034	16.5km (10 miles)	5hrs	168
31	Binn Green to Great Dove Stone Rock	Binn Green SE 017 044	6.5km (4 miles)	2hrs	173
32	Cotton Famine Road	Binn Green SE 017 044	12.5km (7½ miles)	4hrs	176
33	Goyt Valley to Shining Tor	Errwood Reservoir car park SK 013 756	15km (9 miles)	5hrs	182
34	Derbyshire Bridge to Shutlingsloe	Derbyshire Bridge Ranger Centre SK 018 715	20km (12½ miles)	7hrs	187
35	The Roaches	Gradbach car park SJ 998 662	16km (10 miles)	5hrs	193
Long day walks					
36	Marsden to Edale	Marsden SE 049 115/Edale SK 123 857	40km (25 miles)	13hrs	201
37	Langsett to Edale	Langsett Barn SE 211 004/Edale SK 123 857	25km (15½ miles)	8hrs	205
38	Gritstone edges	Fairholmes Visitor Centre SK 172 893/Baslow SK 253 722	45km (28 miles)	13hrs	208
39	Edale Horseshoe	Hope SK 172 834	28km (17½ miles)	8hrs	213
40	Kinder Scout skyline	Birchin Clough SK 109 914	31km (19½ miles)	10hrs	215

APPENDIX B
Useful information

Dark Peak Walking
www.paulbesley.com

For details of the National Park Ranger Offices, transport to and within the Dark Peak, facilities, events and activities, access the Peak District National Park's website www.peakdistrict.gov.uk

For information on accommodation and local events visit www.visitpeakdistrict.com

Peak District National Park Visitor Centres

Castleton
Buxton Road
Castleton
Hope Valley
S33 8WN
tel 01629 816572
castleton@peakdistrict.gov.uk

Edale
Fieldhead
Edale
Hope Valley
S33 7ZA
tel 01433 670207
edale@peakdistrict.gov.uk

Upper Derwent Valley
Fairholmes
Bamford
Hope Valley
S33 0AQ
tel 01433 650953
derwentinfo@peakdistrict.gov.uk

Other useful websites
Moors For The Future
www.moorsforthefuture.org.uk

National Trust
www.nationaltrust.org.uk/features/high-peak-moors-derbyshire

Eastern Moors Partnership
www.visit-eastern-moors.org.uk

The Wildlife Trusts
www.wildlifetrusts.org

British Mountaineering Council
www.thebmc.co.uk

Royal Society for the Protection of Birds
www.rspb.org.uk

YHA
www.yha.org.uk

Mountain Weather Information Service
www.mwis.org.uk

Access
www.openaccess.naturalengland.org.uk

Transport
www.peakdistrict.gov.uk/visiting/publictransport/peakconnections

APPENDIX C

Aircraft crash site locations

There are a number of aircraft crash sites in the Dark Peak within 500 metres of a walk:

Walk	Plane	Year	Grid Reference
Walk 3	Wellington	1942	SK 27100 76969
Walk 4	Wellington	1942	SK 26700 82769
	Blenheim	1941	SK 27900 83770
Walk 7	Vampire	1957	SK 22430 85700
Walk 10	Consul	1951	SK 17499 96673
Walk 13	Defiant	1941	SK 15499 90471
	Meteor	1950	SK 16599 89070
Walk 16	V1 Flying Bomb	1944	SK 18566 96499
	Oxford	1943	SK 18118 96671
Walk 18	Blenheim	1939	SK 08198 97071
	Beaver	1956	SK 05698 97571
	Defiant	1941	SK 10398 97871
	Wellington	1943	SK 10698 98671
Walk 20	Superfortress	1948	SK 09109 94859
	Dakota Skytrain	1945	SK 08022 94744
	Lancaster Bomber	1945	SK 07813 94808
Walk 21	Sabre x 2	1954	SK 07643 90365
Walk 22	Hampden	1942	SK 07898 87470
Walk 23	Wellington	1941	SK 11198 87669
	Wellington	1943	SK 13491 87984
	Halifax	1943	SK 12862 87955
	Dragon Rapide	1963	SK 10298 88270
	Anson	1944	SK 10198 87769
Walk 24	Blenheim	1941	SK 09298 87069
	Harvard	1952	SK 08898 86770
	Anson	1945	SK 08998 86570
Walk 27	Swordfish	1940	SE 08598 04572
Walk 28	Hurricanes x 3	1945	SE 03697 98772
	Lancaster	1948	SE 03497 99271
	Lightning	1944	SE 03397 99672

Walk	Plane	Year	Grid Reference
	Tiger Moth	1944	SF 03497 01472
Walk 30	Dakota	1949	SE 01497 02472
	Lysander	1941	SE 04197 03272
Walk 31	Mosquito	1944	SE 02697 03172
Walk 33	Defiant	N/A	SJ 99831 73577
	Harvard	N/A	SJ 99748 73739
	Oxford	N/A	SJ 99799 74627
	Thunderbolts x 2	N/A	SJ 99501 75393
Walk 34	DeHavilland	N/A	SK 02358 71582
	Oxford	N/A	SK 02555 71718
Walk 36	Liberator	1944	SK 05853 90575
Walk 39	Spitfire	1943	SK 10898 83370
	Thunderbolt	1943	SK 09498 84270
	Oxford	1945	SK 08298 85170
	Oxford	1945	SK 11698 83670
	Hampden	1940	SK 11298 83470

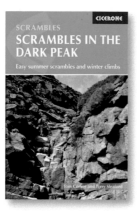
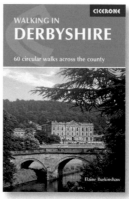

Walking – Trekking – Mountaineering – Climbing – Cycling

Over 40 years, Cicerone have built up an outstanding collection of over 300 guides, inspiring all sorts of amazing adventures.

Every guide comes from extensive exploration and research by our expert authors, all with a passion for their subjects. They are frequently praised, endorsed and used by clubs, instructors and outdoor organisations.

All our titles can now be bought as **e-books**, **ePubs** and **Kindle** files and we also have an online magazine – **Cicerone Extra** – with features to help cyclists, climbers, walkers and trekkers choose their next adventure, at home or abroad.

Our website shows any **new information** we've had in since a book was published. Please do let us know if you find anything has changed, so that we can publish the latest details. On our **website** you'll also find great ideas and lots of detailed information about what's inside every guide and you can buy **individual routes** from many of them online.

It's easy to keep in touch with what's going on at Cicerone by getting our monthly **free e-newsletter**, which is full of offers, competitions, up-to-date information and topical articles. You can subscribe on our home page and also follow us on **Facebook** and **Twitter** or dip into our **blog**.

Cicerone – the very best guides for exploring the world.

CICERONE

Juniper House, Murley Moss, Oxenholme Road, Kendal, Cumbria LA9 7RL
Tel: 015395 62069 info@cicerone.co.uk
www.cicerone.co.uk